W9-BZX-751

ANSWERS TO TOUGH QUESTIONS

JOSH McDOWELL
AND
DON STEWART

THOMAS NELSON PUBLISHERS
Nashville

Published in Nashville, Tennessee, by Thomas Nelson, Inc., Publishers, and distributed in Canada by Word Communications, Ltd., Richmond, British Columbia, and in the United Kingdom by Word (UK), Ltd., Milton Keynes, England.

Scripture quotations noted KJV are from The Holy Bible, KING JAMES VERSION.

Scripture quotations noted NASB are from THE NEW AMERICAN STANDARD BIBLE, Copyright © 1960, 1962, 1963, 1968, 1971, 1972, 1973, 1975, 1977 by The Lockman Foundation and are used by permission.

Scripture quotations noted RSV are from the REVISED STANDARD VERSION of the Bible. Copyright © 1946, 1952, 1971, 1973 by the Division of Christian Education of the National Council of the Churches of Christ in the U.S.A. Used by permission.

Scripture quotations noted MLB and MLVB are from THE MODERN LANGUAGE VERSION BIBLE. Copyright © 1945, 1959, 1959 by Hendrickson Publishers, Peabody, Massachusetts.

Library of Congress Cataloging-in-Publication Data

McDowell, Josh.
    Answers to tough questions skeptics ask about the Christian faith / Josh McDowell and Don Stewart.
        p. cm.
    Originally published: San Bernardino, Calif. : Here's Life Publishers, c1980.
    ISBN 0-8407-4464-1 (pbk.)
    1. Apologetics—20th century—Miscellanea. I. Stewart, Don Douglas. II. Title.
BT1102.M3985 1993
230—dc20   93-27155
                                        CIP

Printed in the United States of America

97 96 95 94 93 — 1 2 3 4 5 6 7 8 9 10

Dedication

The story of Dr. Robert Dick Wilson stands as a remarkable testimony to the reliability of the Bible. Wilson's scholarship, in many ways still unsurpassed, gave the world compelling evidence that the Old Testament is an accurate and trustworthy document. Robert Dick Wilson was born in 1856 in Pennsylvania. In 1886 Wilson received the Doctor's degree. He continued his training at Western Theological Seminary in Pittsburgh, followed by two years in Germany at the University of Berlin.

Upon his arrival in Germany, Professor Wilson made a decision to dedicate his life to the study of the Old Testament. He recounted his decision: "I was twenty-five then; and I judged from the life of my ancestors that I should live to be seventy; so that I should have forty-five years to work. I divided the period into three parts. The first fifteen years I would devote to the study of the languages necessary. For the second fifteen I was going to devote myself to the study of the text of the Old Testament; and I reserved the last fifteen years for the work of writing the results of my previous studies and investigations, so as to give them to the world." Dr. Wilson's plans were carried out almost to the very year he had projected, and his scholastic accomplishments were truly amazing.

As a student in seminary he would read the New Testament in nine different languages including a Hebrew translation which he had memorized syllable for syllable! Wilson also memorized large portions of the Old Testament in the original Hebrew. Incredible as it may seem, Robert Dick Wilson mastered forty-five languages and dialects. Dr. John Walvoord, President of Dallas Theological Seminary, called Dr. Wilson "probably the outstanding authority on ancient languages of the Middle East."

Dr. Wilson commented on his scholastic achievements, relating why he devoted himself to such a monumental task: "Most of our students used to go to Germany, and they heard professors give lectures which were the results of their own labours. The students took everything because the professor said it. I went there to study so that there would be no professor on earth that could lay down the law for me, or say anything without my being able to investigate the evidence on which he said it.

"Now I consider that what was necessary in order to investigate the evidence was, first of all, to know the languages in which the evidence is given. So I . . . determined that I would learn all the languages that throw light upon the Hebrew, and also the languages into which the Bible had been translated down to 600 A.D., so that I could investigate the text myself.

"Having done this I claim to be an expert. I defy any man to make an attack upon the Old Testament on the ground of evidence that I cannot investigate. I can get at the facts if they are linguistic. If you know any language that I do not know, I will learn it."

Wilson challenged other so-called "experts" in the Old Testament field demanding that they prove their qualifications before making statements concerning its history and text. "If a man is called an expert, the first thing to be done is to establish the fact that he is such. One expert may be worth more than a million other witnesses that are not experts. Before a man has the right to speak about the history, the language, and the paleography of the Old Testament, the Christian church has the right to demand that such a man establish his ability to do so."

Dr. Wilson met his own challenge. For forty-six years Wilson had devoted himself to this great task of studying the Old Testament, carefully investigating the evidence that had a bearing upon its historical reliability. Based upon his credentials he was in a better position to speak as an expert than any other man. His findings drove him to the firm conviction that "in the Old Testament we have a true historical account of the history of the Israelite people."

As a professor at Princeton Dr. Wilson won international fame as a scholar and defender of the historic Christian faith. The emphasis of professor Wilson's teaching was to give his students such an intelligent faith in the Old Testament Scriptures that they will never doubt them as long as they live.

He tried to show them that there is reasonable ground for belief in the history of the Old Testament.

Contents

The Bible 📖

Jesus Christ ⤳

God

Miracles Then and Now

Bible Difficulties

World Religions

Christianity ✝

Believing Faith ♥

The Shroud of Turin 🗞

Creation Accounts 🔣

Four Spiritual Laws

About the Authors

Foreword

It is with the greatest satisfaction that I commend to both Christian and non-Christian seekers of truth *Answers* by Josh McDowell and Don Stewart.

Books on Christian apologetics are generally of a dryasdust sort, based on the tradition of Aristotelian-Thomist philosophies (at best) or derivatives of closeminded presuppositionalism (at worst). Such works often do not take the unbeliever's questions seriously—or, even if they do, the answers they give are like the famous preacher who was invisible six days of the week and incomprehensible on the seventh.

In sharp contrast, the present book deals squarely with the live issues on the boundary between faith and unbelief, and is willing to make factual evidence the test of genuine commitment. Again, "evidence is demanding a verdict" and readers will almost inevitably find themselves bringing in that verdict for Jesus Christ.

> — John Warwick Montgomery,
> Ph.D. (Chicago)
> D. Theol. (Strasbourg, France)
> Member of the California and Virginia Bars
> Dean, the Simon Greenleaf School of Law

Introduction

Lecturing on university campuses over the years has given many individuals the opportunity to ask us a variety of questions concerning the validity of Christianity and the Bible. Time has never permitted us the occasion to answer the majority of the questions completely. *Answers to Tough Questions* affords us that opportunity. Explaining many of the sincere inquiries skeptics have about Christianity is the main purpose of this book.

We have tried to deal with as many questions as possible. This means we have by design, been succinct in our answers. For those who desire to go into greater detail there are bibliographic references at the end of most answers.

Answers to Tough Questions will strengthen the faith of the believer and help to answer the inquiries of the non-believer. Sometimes you need to plead ignorance to certain questions because there is simply not enough known about an issue to answer properly. However, one thing that has been learned through years of research is that time is usually on your side. Thanks to archaeology and other disciplines, many of the questions and accusations about Christianity that could not be answered thirty years ago can now be answered with a great deal of certainty.

For the greater part, we have tried to deal mainly with those questions that relate to the credibility of Christianity. Later on we desire to do several more volumes relating to the theological and sociological issues.

What makes the Bible so special?

Christianity believes and teaches that the Bible alone is the revealed Word of God. Even though it was written by men, the ultimate author was God Almighty. This claim was not invented by the Church, but is the claim the Bible makes for itself.

"The word of the Lord endures forever" (I Peter 1:25, MLB). "All Scripture is God-breathed" (II Timothy 3:16, MLB). "For the prophecy came not in old time by the will of man: but holy men of God spake as they were moved by the Holy Ghost" (II Peter 1:21, KJV).

Over 2,000 times in the Old Testament alone there are clauses such as "And God spoke to Moses," "the word of the Lord came unto Jonah," and "God said." Moreover, the Bible claims to be a record of the words and deeds of God, thus the Bible views itself as God's Word.

The mere fact that the Bible claims to be the Word of God does not prove that it is such, for there are other books that make similar claims. The difference is that the Scriptures contain indisputable evidence as being the Word of God.

One reason that the Bible is different from other books is its unity. Although this book was composed by men, its unity betrays the hand of the Almighty. The Bible was written over a period of about 1,500 years by more than forty different human authors. These authors came from a variety of backgrounds, including Joshua (a military general), Daniel (a prime minister), Peter (a fisherman), and Nehemiah (a cupbearer).

The authors of the various books wrote in different places, such as the wilderness (Moses), prison (Paul), and Patmos exile (John). The biblical writings were composed on three different continents (Africa, Asia, and Europe), and in three different languages (Hebrew, Aramaic, and Greek).

The contents of the Bible deal with many controversial subjects. Yet, the Bible is a unity. From beginning to end, there's one unfolding story of God's plan of salvation for mankind. This salvation is through the person of Jesus Christ (John 14:6). Jesus Himself testified that He was the theme of the entire Bible.

"Search the scriptures; for in them ye think ye have eternal life: and they are they which testify of me . . . For had ye believed Moses, ye would have believed me: for he wrote of me. But if ye believe not his writings, how shall ye believe my words?" (John 5:39, 46, 47, KJV).

In another place, "And beginning at Moses and all the prophets, he expounded unto them in all the scriptures the things concerning himself" (Luke 24:27, KJV; see also Luke 24:44).

The Old Testament is the preparation (Isaiah 40:3). The Gospels are the manifestation (John 1:29). The Book of Acts is the propagation (Acts 1:8). The Epistles give the explanation (Colossians 1:27). The Book of Revelation is the consummation (Revelation 1:7). The Bible is all about Jesus.

The entire Bible is a unity with each part needing the others to be complete. Dr. W. F. Albright puts it this way: "To the writers of the New Testament, the Hebrew Bible was Holy Scripture and they were the direct heirs of its prophets. It is, accordingly, quite impossible to understand the New Testament without recognizing that its purpose was to supplement and explain the Hebrew Bible.

"Any attempt to go back to the sources of Christianity without accepting the entire Bible as our guide is thus doomed to failure" (cited by Roger T. Forster and V. Paul Marston, *That's a Good Question*, p. 67).

Lest anyone think this isn't something marvelous, we'd like to give you this challenge. Find ten people from your local area who have similar educational backgrounds, all speak the same language, and all are from basically the same culture, then separate them and ask them to write their opinion on only one controversial subject, such as the meaning of life.

When they have finished, compare the conclusions of these ten writers. Do they agree with each other? Of course not. But the Bible did not consist of merely ten authors, but forty. It was not written in one generation, but over a period of 1,500 years; not by authors with the same education, culture, or language, but with vastly different education, many different cultures, from three continents and three different languages, and finally not just one subject but hundreds.

And yet the Bible is a unity. There is complete harmony, which cannot be explained by coincidence or collusion. The unity of the Bible is a strong argument in favor of its divine inspiration.

The unity of the Scriptures is only one reason among many which supports the Bible's claim to be the divine Word of God. Others which could be explained in detail are the testimony of the early Church, the witness of history and archaeology, and the evidence of changed lives throughout the centuries, to name but a few.

These factors led the great archaeologist, W. F. Albright, to conclude, "The Bible towers in content above all earlier religious literature; and it towers just as impressively over all subsequent literature in the direct simplicity of its message and the catholicity of its appeal to men of all lands and times" (*The Christian Century*, November, 1958).

The Bible is special. It is unique. No other book has any such credentials. No other book even comes close. "England has two books, the Bible and Shakespeare. England made Shakespeare, but the Bible made England" (Victor Hugo, cited by Mead, *Encyclopedia of Religious Quotations*, p. 49).

✚ ADDITIONAL REFERENCE SOURCES

Josh McDowell, *Evidence That Demands a Verdict*, rev. ed., Here's Life Publishers, 1979

Norman Geisler and William Nix, *A General Introduction to the Bible,*. Moody Press, 1973

Don Stewart, "The Seven Wonders of the Bible" (tape), The Word for Today, P.O. Box 8000, Costa Mesa, CA 92626

Q Hasn't the New Testament been changed since it has been copied and recopied throughout history?

A A common misconception is that the text of the Bible has not come down to us the way in which it was originally written. Accusations abound of zealous monks changing the biblical text throughout Church history. This issue is of the utmost importance, since an altered text would do grave damage to the credibility of the story.

As F. F. Bruce says, "The historical 'once-for-all-ness' of Christianity which distinguishes it from those religious and philosophical systems, which are not specially related to any particular time, makes the reliability of the writings which purport to record this revelation a question of first-rate importance" (*The New Testament Documents: Are They Reliable?* p. 8).

Fortunately, the problem is not a lack of evidence. There are three different types of evidence that are to be used in evaluating the New Testament text. These are the Greek manuscripts, the various versions in which the New Testament is translated, and the writings of the Church fathers.

The New Testament was originally composed in the Greek language. There are approximately 5,500 copies in existence that contain all or part of the New Testament. Although we do not possess the originals, copies exist from a very early date.

The New Testament was written from about A.D. 50 to A.D. 90. The earliest fragment (p. 52) dates about A.D. 120, with about fifty other fragments dating within 150–200 years from the time of composition.

Two major manuscripts, Codex Vaticanus (A.D. 325) and Codex Sinaiticus (A.D. 350), a complete copy, date within 250 years of the time of composition. This may seem like a long time span, but it is minimal compared to most ancient works.

The earliest copy of Caesar's *The Gallic Wars* dates 1,000 years after it was written, and the first complete copy of the *Odyssey* by Homer dates 2,200 years after it was written. When the interval between the writing of the New Testament and earliest copies is compared to other ancient works, the New Testament proves to be much closer to the time of the original.

The 5,500 copies are far and away the most we have of any ancient work. Many ancient writings have been transmitted to us by only a handful of manuscripts (Catullus—three copies; the earliest one is 1,600 years after he wrote; Herodotus—eight copies and 1,300 years).

Not only do the New Testament documents have more manuscript evidence and close time interval between the writing and earliest copy, but they were also translated into several other languages at an early date. Translation of a document into another language was rare in the ancient world, so this is an added plus for the New Testament.

The number of copies of the versions is in excess of 18,000, with possibly as many as 25,000. This is further evidence that helps us establish the New Testament text.

Even if we did not possess the 5,500 Greek manuscripts or the 18,000 copies of the versions, the text of the New Testament could still be reproduced within 250 years from its composition. How? By the writings of the early Christians. In commentaries, letters, etc., these ancient writers quote the biblical text, thus giving us another witness to the text of the New Testament.

John Burgon has catalogued more than 86,000 citations by the early church fathers who cite different parts of the New Testament. Thus we observe that there is so much more evidence for the reliability of the New Testament text than any other comparable writings in the ancient world.

F. F. Bruce makes the following observation: "The evidence for our New Testament writings is ever so much greater than the evidence for many writings of classical authors, the authenticity of which no one dreams of questioning."

He also states, "And if the New Testament were a collection of secular writings, their authenticity would generally be regarded as beyond all doubt" (*The New Testament Documents: Are They Reliable?* p. 15).

Sir Frederic Kenyon, former director and principal librarian of the British Museum, was one of the foremost experts on ancient manuscripts and their authority. Shortly before his death, he wrote this concerning the New Testament:

"The interval between the dates of original composition (of the New Testament) and the earliest extant evidence becomes so small as to be in fact negligible, and the last foundation for any doubt that the Scriptures have come down to us substantially as they were written has now been removed. Both the authenticity and the general integrity of the books of the New Testament may be regarded as finally established" (*The Bible and Archaeology*, pp. 288-89).

✚ ADDITIONAL REFERENCE SOURCES

F. F. Bruce, *The New Testament Documents: Are They Reliable?* rev. ed., Eerdmans, 1977

John Warwick Montgomery, *History and Christianity*, Here's Life Publishers, 1983

Josh McDowell, *Evidence That Demands a Verdict*, rev. ed., Here's Life Publishers, 1979

Colin Brown (ED), *History, Criticism, and Faith*, 2nd ed., Inter-Varsity Press, July, 1977

How can anyone believe the New Testament account of the life of Jesus, seeing that it was written long after His death?

There seems to be some type of general consensus among many people that the New Testament documents were written many years after the events took place and hence do not contain reliable information. However, the fact of the matter is that the life of Jesus was written by eyewitnesses or people who recorded firsthand testimony. The writers were all living at the same time these events transpired, and they had personal contact either with the events or with people who witnessed the events.

There is strong internal testimony that the Gospels were written at an early date. The Book of Acts records the missionary activity of the early Church and was written as a sequel by the same person who wrote the Gospel according to Luke. The Book of Acts ends with the apostle Paul being alive in Rome, his death not being recorded.

This would lead us to believe that it was written before he died, since the other major events in his life have been recorded. We have some reason to believe that Paul was put to death in the Neronian persecution of A.D. 64, which means the Book of Acts was composed before this time.

If the Book of Acts was written before A.D. 64, then the Gospel of Luke, to which Acts was a sequel, had to have been composed some time before that, probably in the late fifties or early sixties of the first century. The death of Christ took place around A.D. 30, which would make the composition of Luke at the latest within thirty years of the events.

The early Church generally taught that the first Gospel composed was that of Matthew, which would place us still closer to the time of Christ. This evidence leads us to believe that the first three Gospels were all composed within thirty years from the time these events occurred, a time when unfriendly eyewitnesses were still living who could contradict their testimony if it was not accurate.

This type of evidence has recently led one liberal scholar, John A.T. Robinson, to re-date the New Testament documents much earlier than most modern liberal scholars would have us believe. Robinson has argued in *Redating the New Testament* that the entire New Testament could have been completed before A.D. 70, which is still well into the eyewitness period.

Facts involved in the issue led W. F. Albright, the great biblical archaeologist, to comment, "We can already say emphatically that there is no longer any solid basis for dating any book of the New Testament after A.D. 80, two full generations before the date between 130 and 150 given by the more radical New Testament critics of today" (William F. Albright, *Recent Discoveries in Bible Lands*, New York, Funk and Wagnalls, 1955, p. 136).

Albright's A.D. 80 date might be questioned when it comes to the Gospel of John. There is a strong possibility the apostle John's banishment to Patmos under Domitian was as late as A.D. 95–96 in Revelation 1. There is strong tradition John wrote Revelation there at that time. This is testified to by Clement of Alexandria, Eusebius, and Irenaeus (cf. *New Testament Survey*, p. 391, by Robert Gromacki).

The evidence points out that (1) the documents were not written long after the events but within close proximity to them, and (2) they were written by people during the period when many who were acquainted with the facts or were eyewitnesses to them were still living. The inescapable conclusion is that the New Testament picture of Christ can be trusted.

✚   ADDITIONAL REFERENCE SOURCES

F. F. Bruce, *The New Testament Documents: Are They Reliable?* rev. ed., Eerdman, 1977

John A.T. Robinson, *Redating the New Testament*, London, SCM Press, 1976

A. N. Sherwin-White, *Roman Society and Roman Law in the New Testament*, Oxford, Claredon, 1963

Gerhard Maier, *The End of the Historical-Critical Method*, Concordia, 1977

John Warwick Montgomery, *History and Christianity*, Here's Life Publishers, 1983

Why do some people say that Mark was the first Gospel written?

The theory that Mark's Gospel was the first to be written is based upon several arguments. Most of the material contained in Mark (about 93%) can be found in Matthew and Luke. It is easier for some to believe that Matthew and Luke expanded Mark rather than that Mark abbreviated Matthew and Luke.

Sometimes Matthew and Luke agree with Mark in the actual words used, but they never agree with each other when differing from Mark. This would seem to prove that both Matthew and Luke depended upon Mark to get their information.

The order of events in Mark seems to be original. Wherever Matthew's order differs from Mark, the Gospel of Luke supports Mark's order, and whenever Luke differs from Mark's order, Matthew agrees with Mark. This shows that Mark was composed first, and that Matthew and Luke are merely following his order, seeing that they never agree with each other against Mark.

Mark also reveals a primitive nature when compared to the other two Gospels. Mark, for example, uses the word *kurie* (Lord) only one time while Matthew employs it nineteen times and Luke sixteen times. This fact indicates an attitude of reverence which eventually developed in the later Gospels.

The above are some of the arguments that scholars use to suggest that Mark was composed first. However, upon closer inspection, these reasons are not as strong as some might think.

It is possible that Mark condensed his Gospel for reasons beyond our knowledge. The material which the Gospels have in common might be a result of a common oral tradition. It is entirely possible that Mark never did see Matthew or Luke before he wrote his Gospel, and it is also conceivable that none of the Gospel writers saw any of the other three writings before their works were composed.

As for Matthew and Luke never agreeing word for word against Mark in parallel passages, there can be found passages where they agree where Mark contains something different, showing non-dependence on Mark.

The idea of Mark's order being original is not as obvious as some imply. Mark may have worked from Matthew and Luke, following their order when the two agreed, but deciding to follow one or the other when they did not appear to agree.

The matter of *kurie* (Lord) being a reverential term is open to question, since Matthew uses it seven times when referring to a mere man (13:27; 21:29; 25:11, 20, 22, 24; 27:63), showing it was not a term used only for God.

This demonstrates that a chronology cannot be erected by the use or non-use of this term. To this can be added the fact that the early Church, which was closer to the situation, unanimously opted for the priority of Matthew's composition, there being no evidence that Mark wrote first.

Moreover, there are some telling reasons against the theory of Markan priority. Matthew was an eyewitness. It seems unnecessary to assume that he depended upon Mark, who was not an eyewitness, to gather his information on the life of Christ, including Matthew's own conversion!

The theory also fails to explain why Luke omitted any mention of Mark 6:45–8:26 if he used Mark as a source. This is a very important section, and the easiest solution is to surmise that Luke did not have Mark's Gospel before him while composing his work.

The two-source theory does not adequately explain why Matthew and Luke agree in certain sections where Mark has something else.

The theory of the priority of Mark is anything but an established fact.

✚ ADDITIONAL REFERENCE SOURCES

Donald Guthrie, *New Testament Introduction*, 3rd rev. ed., Inter-Varsity Press, 1970

Simon Kistemaker, *The Gospels in Current Study*, Baker Book House, 1972

A.H. McNeile, *An Introduction to the Study of the New Testament*, London, Oxford Univ. Press, 1953

Merrill Tenney, *The Genius of the Gospels*, Eerdmans, 1951

What is Q?

One of the most popular theories in New Testament study is that the Gospel of Mark was written first, and that both Matthew and Luke were based upon Mark and another source called "Q" which no longer exists. "Q" comes from the German word "quelle" meaning source, and it supposedly contained matters in Matthew and Luke that are not found in Mark.

The idea of a "Q" source is a relatively recent development in New Testament study. In modern times, Matthew, Mark, and Luke have been referred to as the "synoptic Gospels," since they take a similar view of the life of Christ.

Many presuppose that the extensive agreements between these Gospels indicate some type of literary collaboration, and for the last century New Testament scholars have been attempting to explain this phenomenon. One factor that complicates matters is that there are many instances in which one Gospel describes matters differently from either one or both of the other Gospels.

The quest for a solution as to how these similarities and dissimilarities occurred is known as the "synoptic problem," while "source criticism" is the field of study devoted to solving the problem.

The early church was not too concerned with this problem, assuming that the Gospel writers recorded their information from personal memory and firsthand reports as opposed to the need of copying each other or a common written source.

Matthew was the first Gospel to have been composed, according to the testimony of Eusebius, an early church writer.

Eusebius relates that Matthew wrote down his Gospel as he was about to leave the land of Palestine. His account was largely drawn from his own experience as a disciple of Christ.

Clement of Alexandria says that Mark based his Gospel on the reminiscence of Peter, while Luke testifies that his work was drawn from a number of sources (Luke 1:1–4).

Even though there was almost universal testimony among the early scholars as to the priority of Matthew, the nineteenth century saw the emergence of the theory of Mark being written first, or "Markan priority." Most books written on the synoptic problem today assert this theory. Thus the need arises for the two-source theory, Mark and "Q," to explain the material found in Matthew and Luke but not in Mark.

There is good reason to question this theory that Matthew and Luke used "Q" in the Gospel of Mark as sources. First, no such document "Q" has ever been found. Second, there is no agreement of exactly what sayings should be in "Q." Third, there is no historical testimony for the existence of a Q-type document by historian or writer. And fourth, as pointed out, the weight of historical evidence does not point to Mark as being the first Gospel written, which is imperative for this theory.

✚ ADDITIONAL REFERENCE SOURCES

William R. Farmer, *The Synoptic Problem: A Critical Analysis*, Dillsboro, Western North Carolina Press, 1976

George Ladd, *The New Testament and Criticism*, Eerdmans, 1967

Simon Kistemaker, *The Gospels in Current Study*, Baker, 1972

Ned B. Stonehouse, *Origins of the Synoptic Gospels*, Eerdmans, 1963

Donald Guthrie, *New Testament Introduction*, 3rd rev. ed., Inter-Varsity Press, 1970

There are so many different interpretations of the Bible, why should I believe yours?

One of the complaints we often hear is that everyone has a different interpretation of the Bible. Because many people arrive at varying conclusions when they read the Bible, there is supposedly no way to get a consensus. People point to the variety of denominations as an example that there can be no unanimity of agreement between Bible believers.

This idea neglects to take into account certain facts. The great majority of Bible readers have no problem with agreement on the central teachings of the Bible. Even those who do not believe the Bible to be true have no difficulty whatsoever discerning the main message.

Within all branches of Christianity, we find the same basic understanding as to what the Bible teaches. They usually accept the same creeds that assert such basic truths as that God made man in His image, with freedom of choice, and that man chose to rebel against God, thus bringing sin into the world.

God, because of His everlasting love, became a man in the person of Jesus Christ and died a substitutionary death on our behalf, paying the penalty for sin. Mankind can have their relationship restored with God through placing their faith in Jesus Christ.

The message of the Bible is clear for those who will read it and seek to find out its meaning. The problem comes when people bring their preconceived notions to the Bible and attempt to make the Word fit their preconceived ideas. This is not the fault of the Bible, but of the persons who force the Bible to say whatever they want it to say.

As for the matter of the various denominations, it must be stressed that they are not formed because of division over the central teachings of Christianity. The differences are a result of a variety of factors, including cultural, ethnic, and social. When closely compared with one another, the doctrinal differences are not always that crucial.

Some people use this argument as an excuse for not believing in Jesus, but like all others it does not prove to be valid. Jesus made the main issue crystal clear, "He who believes in the Son has eternal life; but he who does not obey the Son shall not see life, but the wrath of God abides on him" (John 3:36, NASB). Often the disagreement is not so much with the interpretation of the Scriptures, but rather with the application.

✚ ADDITIONAL REFERENCE SOURCES

Bernard Ramm, *Protestant Biblical Interpretation*, Baker, 1970

R. C. Sproul, *Knowing Scripture*, Inter-Varsity Press, 1977

I. Howard Marshall (Ed.), *New Testament Interpretation*, Eerdmans, 1977

How can you believe a Bible that is full of contradictions?

It is truly amazing how often this question is asked. This question contains the assumption that the Bible is filled with many obvious discrepancies which, if true, would make it impossible to believe that the Bible has a divine origin. It is a popular idea to maintain that the Bible disagrees with itself, which casts considerable doubt on its trustworthiness.

If, indeed, the Bible does contain demonstrable errors, it would show that at least those parts could not have come from a perfect, all-knowing God. We do not argue with this conclusion, but we do disagree with the initial premise that the Scriptures are full of mistakes. It is very easy to accuse the Bible of inaccuracies, but it is quite another matter to prove it.

Certain passages at first glance appear to be contradictory, but further investigation will show that this is not the case.

One of the things for which we appeal with regard to possible contradictions is fairness. We should not minimize or exaggerate the problem, and we must always begin by giving the author the benefit of the doubt. This is the rule in other literature, and we ask that it also be the rule here. We find so often that people want to employ a different set of rules when it comes to examining the Bible, and to this we immediately object.

What constitutes a contradiction? The law of non-contradiction, which is the basis of all logical thinking, states that a thing cannot be both *a* and *non-a* at the same time. In other words, it cannot be both raining and not raining at the same time.

If one can demonstrate a violation of this principle from Scripture, then and only then can he prove a contradiction. For example, if the Bible said—which it does not—that Jesus died by crucifixion both at Jerusalem and at Nazareth at the same time, this would be a provable error.

When facing possible contradictions, it is of the highest importance to remember that two statements may differ from each other without being contradictory. Some fail to make a distinction between contradiction and difference.

For example, the case of the blind men at Jericho. Matthew relates how two blind men met Jesus, while both Mark and Luke mention only one. However, neither of these statement denies the other, but rather they are complementary.

Suppose you were talking to the mayor of your city and the chief of police at city hall. Later, you see your friend, Jim, and tell him you talked to the mayor today. An hour later, you see your friend, John, and tell him you talked to both the mayor and the chief of police.

When your friends compare notes, there is a seeming contradiction. But there is no contradiction. If you had told Jim that you talked *only* to the mayor, you would have contradicted that statement by what you told John.

The statements you actually made to Jim and John are different, but not contradictory. Likewise, many biblical statements fall into this category. Many think they find errors in passages that they have not correctly read.

In the Book of Judges we have the account of the death of Sisera. Judges 5:25–27 is supposed to represent Jael as having slain him with her hammer and tent peg while he was drinking milk. Judges 4:21 says she did it while he was asleep. However, a closer reading of Judges 5:25–27 will reveal that it is not stated that he was drinking milk at the moment of impact. Thus, the discrepancy disappears.

Sometimes two passages appear to be contradictory because the translation is not as accurate as it could be. A knowledge of the original languages of the Bible can immediately solve these difficulties, for both Greek and Hebrew—as all languages—have their peculiarities that make them difficult to render into English or any other language.

A classic example concerns the accounts of Paul's conversion as recorded in the Book of Acts. Acts 9:7 (KJV) states, "The men which journeyed with him stood speechless, hearing a voice, but seeing no man." Acts 22:9 (KJV) reads, "And they that were with me saw indeed the light, and were afraid; but they heard not the voice of him that spake to me."

These statements seem contradictory, with one saying that Paul's companions heard a voice, while the other account says that no voice was heard. However, a knowledge of Greek solves this difficulty. As the Greek scholar, W. F. Arndt, explains:

"The construction of the verb 'to hear' (*akouo*) is not the same in both accounts. In Acts 9:7 it is used with the genitive, in Acts 22:9 with the accusative. The construction with the genitive simply expresses that something is being heard or that certain sounds reach the ear; nothing is indicated as to whether a person understands what he hears or not.

"The construction with the accusative, however, describes a hearing which includes mental apprehension of the message spoken. From this it becomes evident that the two passages are not contradictory.

"Acts 22:9 does not deny that the associates of Paul heard certain sounds; it simply declares that they did not hear in such a way as to understand what was being said. Our English idiom in this case simply is not so expressive as the Greek" (*Does the Bible Contradict Itself*, pp. 13–14.)

It must also be stressed that when a possible explanation is given to a Bible difficulty, it is unreasonable to state that the passage contains a demonstrable error. Some difficulties in Scripture result from our inadequate knowledge about the circumstances, and do not necessarily involve an error. These only prove that we are ignorant of the background.

As historical and archaeological study proceed, new light is being shed on difficult portions of Scripture and many "errors" have disappeared with the new understanding. We need a wait-and-see attitude on some problems.

While all Bible difficulties and discrepancies have not yet been cleared up, it is our firm conviction that as more knowledge is gained of the Bible's past, these problems will fade away. The biblical conception of God is an all-knowing, all-pow-

erful being who does not contradict Himself, and so we feel
that His Word, when properly understood, will not contradict
itself.

✚ ADDITIONAL REFERENCE SOURCES

W. F. Arndt, *Does the Bible Contradict Itself?*, 5th rev. ed., Concordia Press,
 1955

John J. Davis, *Biblical Numerology*, Bake Book House, 1968

John W. Haley, *Alleged Discrepancies of the Bible*, reprinted, Baker Book
 House, Grand Rapids, 1977

W. F. Arndt, *Bible Difficulties*, Concordia Press, St. Louis, 1971

Most people say Moses didn't write the first five books of the Bible. What do you say?

Although the mosaic authorship of the Pentateuch (the first five books of the Bible) has been challenged for the past century and a half, there is still good reason to believe it to be true.

It has become fashionable to believe that the Pentateuch is a result of a compilation of various documents labeled J, E, D, P, which were eventually put together by an editor in its present form about 400 B.C. This fanciful and elaborate theory, however, has little to recommend it and is based upon erroneous methods of investigation.

As C. S. Lewis illustrates from personal experience, when he writes about the critics' application of their methods to his words:

"What forearms me against all these Reconstructions is the fact that I have seen it all from the other end of the stick. I have watched reviewers reconstructing the genesis of my own books in just this way.

"Until you come to be reviewed yourself you would never believe how little of an ordinary review is taken up by criticism in the strict sense: by evaluation, praise or censure of the book actually written. Most of it is taken up with imaginary histories of the process by which you wrote it.

"The very terms which the reviewers use in praising or dispraising often imply such a history. They praise a passage as 'spontaneous' and censure another as 'labored'; that is, they think they know that you wrote the one *currente calamo* and the other *invita Minerva*.

"What the value of such reconstructions is I learned very early in my career. I had published a book of essays; and the one into which I had put most of my heart, the one I really cared about and in which I discharged a keen enthusiasm, was on William Morris. And in almost the first review I was told that this was obviously the only one in the book in which I had felt no interest.

"Now don't mistake. The critic was, I now believe, quite right in thinking it the worst essay in the book; at least everyone agreed with him. Where he was totally wrong was in his imaginary history of the causes which produced its dullness.

"Well, this made me prick up my ears. Since then I have watched with some care imaginary histories both of my own books and of books by friends whose real history I knew.

"Reviewers, both friendly and hostile, will dash you off such histories with great confidence; will tell you what public events had directed the author's mind to this or that, what other authors had influenced him, what his over-all intention was, what sort of audience he principally addressed, why— and when—he did everything.

"Now I must first record my impression; then, distinct from it, what I can say with certainty. My impression is that in the whole of my experience not one of these guesses has on any one point been right; that the method shows a record of 100 percent failure.

"You would expect that by mere chance they would hit as often as they miss. But it is my impression that they do no such thing. I can't remember a single hit. But as I have not kept a careful record, my mere impressions may be mistaken. What I think I can say with certainty is that they are usually wrong . . ." (*Christian Reflections*, p. 159–160).

It must be initially stated that Moses was in a position to write the Pentateuch. He was educated in the royal court of Egypt, which was highly advanced academically. He had first-hand knowledge of the geography of Egypt and the Sinai, with plenty of time—forty years in wandering and forty more years beyond that—to compose his work. At the same time that Moses lived, there were uneducated slaves working in the

Egyptian turquoise mines writing on the walls, thus demonstrating the extent of writing in Moses' day.

The evidence within the Pentateuch points to Mosaic authorship, since it clearly portrays Moses as the author of certain portions. "And Moses wrote all the words of the LORD" (Exodus 24:4, KJV). "And he took the book of the covenant, and read in the audience of the people" (Exodus 24:7, KJV). "And the Lord said to Moses, 'Write these words; in accordance with these words I have made a covenant with you and with Israel'" (Exodus 34:27, RSV). To these references many others could be added.

Not only does the internal evidence of the Scriptures make it clear that Moses wrote the Pentateuch, but other Old Testament books make Mosaic authorship clear. Joshua 8:32 (KJV) refers to "the law of Moses, which he wrote." Additional Old Testament references include I Kings 2:3, II Kings 14:6, and Joshua 23:6, which attribute to Moses the authorship of the Pentateuch.

Jewish tradition is firm in its belief in Mosaic authorship. Ecclesiasticus, one of the books of the apocrypha, written about 180 B.C., states, "All this is the covenant-book of God Most High, the Law which Moses enacted to be the heritage of the assemblies of Jacob" (Ecclesiasticus 24:23). The Talmud, in Baba Bathra, 146, which is a Jewish commentary on the first five books (around 200 B.C.), along with the writings of Flavius Josephus (born A.D. 37) and philo (A.D. 20) also concur.

Early Christian tradition likewise agrees that Moses composed the Pentateuch. The writings of Junilius (A.D. 527–565) and Leontius of Byzantium (sixth century A.D.) along with Church fathers Melito (A.D. 175), Cyril of Jerusalem (A.D. 348–386), and Hilary (A.D. 366) teach that Moses wrote the Pentateuch.

Add to this the testimony of the New Testament. The apostles believed that "Moses wrote unto us" (Mark 12:19, KJV) as did the apostle Paul, who when speaking of a passage in the Pentateuch said, "Moses describeth" (Romans 10:5, KJV).

However, the issue as to the authorship of the first five books is once-and-for-all solved by the testimony of the God-man Jesus Christ. Jesus made it clear that Moses wrote these books (Mark 7:10; 10:3–5; 12:26; Luke 5:14; 16:29–31; 24:27, 44; John 7:19, 23).

In John 5:45–47, Jesus states, "Do not think that I will accuse you before the Father; the one who accuses you is Moses, in whom you have set your hope. For if you believed Moses, you would believe Me; for he wrote of Me. But if you do not believe his writings, how will you believe My words?" (NASB).

Two other considerations to be taken into account when examining the evidence with regard to those who do not believe that Moses wrote the Pentateuch are their view of the world and archaeology.

Those who advocate that Moses is not the author usually hold to the idea that there is no supernatural work of God in the world, nor has there ever been. Thus, it would be foolish to believe all the historical information written about the creation of the world, the crossing of the Red Sea, God speaking to Moses, or even the historical evidence that Moses, a prophet of God, wrote the account in the first place. The whole idea is more of a story.

What they fail to do is consider the evidence because of their view of the world. This type of reasoning is faulty. First, one examines the evidence and then decides his case. Simply examining the evidence doesn't mean one will agree with someone else's conclusions, but it does mean he is not rejecting the conclusions out of ignorance.

Second, in the past fifty years archaeological finds have vindicated many of the Old Testament claims supporting the probability of Mosaic authorship. This is because most all of the finds demonstrate that only someone who lived during the time the Bible purports that Moses lived could have known and written about the things in these books.

When all this evidence is considered together, the Mosaic authorship of the Pentateuch is shown to be a fact. Such primary evidence would be accepted without hesitation in a court of law, and any theory of multiple documents would be ruled out as inadmissible. There is simply no evidence to support that theory which cannot be very reasonably answered.

✚ ADDITIONAL REFERENCE SOURCES

Umberto Cassuto, *The Documentary Hypothesis*, 1st English ed., Jerusalem Magnes Press, 1961

Gleason Archer, *A Survey of Old Testament Introduction*, rev. ed., Moody Press, 1979

Josh McDowell, *More Evidence that Demands A Verdict*, Campus Crusade for Christ, 1975

Robert Dick Wilson, "Is the Higher Criticism Scholarly?" Reprinted in *Which Bible?*

How could Moses have written the Book of Deuteronomy when it contains the account of his death?

Though orthodox Christians and Jews alike argue that Moses wrote the first five books of the Old Testament, some people deny his authorship of the fifth book, Deuteronomy. They do this partly on the grounds that chapter 34 contains the account of Moses' death.

Since no one can write an account of his own death, they argue, doesn't this mean the Book of Deuteronomy had to have been written later than the time of Moses?

Probably some orthodox Christians and Jews would attempt to argue that all of chapter 34 in Deuteronomy was written by Moses, although it is possible that the chapter was prophetic. A more plausible explanation is to assume that it was written after the death of Moses, by Joshua. This does not force one to attribute the rest of Deuteronomy to someone besides Moses.

It is quite common that an obituary is placed at the end of a final work by a great author. It would be amazing if the death of Moses weren't recorded, seeing that his entire life otherwise had been told in great detail. The appearance of the account of Moses' death in no way affects his authorship of the preceding 33 chapters.

✚ ADDITIONAL REFERENCE SOURCES

Gleason Archer, *A Survey of Old Testament Introduction*, rev. ed., Moody Press, 1979

R.K. Harrison, *Introduction to the Old Testament*, Eerdmans, 1970

Q Does archaeological evidence prove the Bible? How do archaeological discoveries relate to events in Scripture?

A Archaeology is the study of non-perishable debris, the rubbish man has left behind him that has survived the ravages of time. The initial motivation for digging up ancient civilizations was the desire for buried treasure.

Today, however, the most modern scientific methods are used to recover the study the remains of the past in order to achieve a better understanding of ancient people and their practices. The Middle East, particularly the Palestinian area, is the subject of many archaeological excavations because of its continuous history.

It is important to note that archaeology without history is meaningless. All that archaeology can tell us is a sequence of cultural development, not give us an exact chronology. History gives us the chronology, the events, people, places.

What archaeology has done in the past 100 years is to verify some of the history contained in the Bible. For instance, two of the cities mentioned in the Bible, Sodom and Gomorrah, have been for many years considered mythological.

However, recent excavations at Tell Mardikh, now known to be the site of Ebla, uncovered about 15,000 tablets. Some of these have been translated, and mention is made of Sodom and Gomorrah.

Other archaeological verifications include proof that there was a ruler named Belshazzar; the Hittites not only existed but also had a vast empire; King Sargon also ruled; and the matters that touch upon history in the Book of Acts are demonstrably accurate. So far, the findings of archaeology have verified, and in no case disputed, historical points of the biblical record.

While archaeology can verify history and shed light on various passages of the Bible, it is beyond the realm of archaeology to prove the Bible is the Word of God. At present, archaeology is an improving science, with limited data available, but even with its limitations this discipline is very helpful in illustrating that many biblical passages are historically accurate.

One cannot stress too strongly the importance of the Bible giving an accurate historical picture. Christianity is a historical faith which claims that God has broken into history with many mighty acts.

Although the miracles recorded in Scripture cannot be scientifically tested or repeated due to their nature, persons, places, and events can be investigated historically. If the biblical writers were incorrect in their historical picture, serious doubt would then be cast upon their trustworthiness in areas which couldn't be verified.

Putting it another way, if the authors of Scripture are accurate in their accounts of the things that transpired, it then follows that they cannot be ruled out of court because they happen to mention things out of the ordinary.

✚   ADDITIONAL REFERENCE SOURCES

Donald J. Wiseman and Edwin M. Yamauchi, *Archaeology and the Bible*, Zondervan Publishing Company, 1979

Josh McDowell, *More Evidence That Demands a Verdict*, Campus Crusade for Christ, 1975, pp. 17-22, 301-322

Joseph Free, *Archaeology and Bible History*, rev. ed., Wheaton, Scripture Press, 1969

Clifford Wilson, *Rocks, Relics and Biblical Reliability*, Grand Rapids, Zondervan, 1977

Clifford Wilson, *Ebla Tablets: Secrets of a Forgotten City*, San Diego, Master Books (Division CLP), 1979

How do the Dead Sea Scrolls relate to biblical criticism?

In the 1948 printing of his excellent book Our Bible and Ancient Manuscripts, Sir Frederic Kenyon, the textual scholar, had this to say, "There is indeed no probability that we shall find manuscripts of the Hebrew text going back to a period before the formation of the text which we know as Massoretic. We can only arrive at an idea of it by a study of the earliest translations made from it . . ." (cited by Pfeiffer, The Dead Sea Scrolls and the Bible, p. 107).

At the same time his book was being printed, discoveries began in 1947 that would render any further statements like Kenyon's impossible. Until this time, scholars had only the clay tablets of Babylon and the Egyptian papyri to help them understand background information on the Bible, since no ancient Old Testament manuscripts were known to have survived.

However, all that changed with a discovery of some scrolls in caves along the northwest corner of the Dead Sea. These scrolls brought to the world manuscripts of Old Testament books 1,000 years older than any previously in existence.

There was immediate excitement over the find. Dr. William F. Albright, one of the world's leading archaeologists, in a letter to John Trever who had an integral part in revealing the find, said:

"My heartiest congratulations on the greatest manuscript discovery of modern times! There is no doubt in my mind that the script is more archaic than that of the Nash papyrus (a very small portion of the Old Testament dated between the second century B.C. and first century A.D.) . . . I would prefer a date around 100 B.C. . . .

"What an absolutely incredible find! And there can be happily not the slightest doubt in the world about the genuineness of the manuscript."

Before the discovery of these scrolls, the oldest complete copy of the Old Testament in Hebrew was Codex Babylonicus Petropalitanus from A.D. 1008, more than 1,400 years after the Old Testament was completed. Fragments from the Dead Sea Scrolls now closed the gap by a thousand years and left the world waiting to see if the text had been transmitted accurately. The answer was a resounding *yes*.

The Dead Sea Scrolls demonstrated unequivocally the fact that the Jews were faithful in their transcription of biblical manuscripts. This reverence for the Scriptures was summed up long ago by the first century Jewish historian, Flavius Josephus:

"We have given practical proof of our reverence for our own Scriptures. For, although such long ages have now passed, no one has ventured either to add, or to remove, or to alter a syllable; and it is an instinct with every Jew from the day of his birth to regard them as the decrees of God, to abide by them, and, if need be, cheerfully die for them.

"Time and again ere now, the sight has been witnessed of prisoners enduring tortures and death in every form in the theaters, rather than utter a single word against the Laws and the allied documents" ("Flavius Josephus Against Apion," in *Josephus, Complete Works*, translated by William Whiston, Grand Rapids, Kregel Pub., 1960, p. 179, 180).

The attitude that Josephus related is borne out by the comparison of the Massoretic text, which is the basis of our Hebrew Bibles, and the scrolls from the Dead Sea. Among the fragments discovered are complete copies or parts of every Old Testament book except Esther, and the variations in the text after a thousand years of copying are minimal. Thus any appeal to the Dead Sea Scrolls as casting doubt on the Bible's reliability is invalid.

Charles Pfeiffer had this to say along that line, "It should be noted that, while negative higher critical views of the Bible cannot be refuted by a study of the Qumran scrolls (Qumran is the main location in the Dead Sea area where the scrolls were found), there is no evidence from Qumran to justify a major reassessment of the traditional views of the origin of biblical writings.

"The Old Testament books from Qumran are those which we find in our Bibles. Minor textual variants occur as they do in any document which depends on hand copies for multiplication, but the biblical text may be regarded as essentially reliable" (*The Dead Sea Scrolls and the Bible*, Charles F. Pfeiffer, Baker Book House, 1967, p. 114).

Therefore, the discovery of the Dead Sea Scrolls only supports the critical but conservative approach to the Old Testament as scholars of this persuasion uphold upon studying the reliability of the Old Testament books.

✚ ADDITIONAL REFERENCE SOURCES

William Sanford La Sor, *The Dead Sea Scrolls and the New Testament*, Grand Rapids, Eerdmans, 1972

J. T. Milik, *Ten Years of Discovery in the Wilderness of Judea*, Allenson, 1959

Geza Vermes, *The Dead Sea Scrolls: Qumran in Perspective*, Collins, 1978

Roland De Vaux, *Archaeology and the Dead Sea Scrolls*, Oxford University Press, 1973

Charles F. Pfeiffer, *The Dead Sea Scrolls and the Bible*, Baker Book House, 1967

How many Isaiahs were there?

This is a highly complex question, and an answer less than book length barely scratches the surface. There has been more discussion of the unity of Isaiah by both defenders and critics than any other prophetic book of the Old Testament.

It is the unanimous opinion of the critical school of thought that the Book of Isaiah is not a unity. Chapters 40–66 are supposedly written by an unknown author or authors living at the end of the Babylonian captivity (after 540 B.C.) and are designated as Deutero-Isaiah or Second Isaiah.

Many overlapping and equally unfounded lines of argument are used to support this contention. The critics contend that chapters 40–66 presuppose the exile. The city of Jerusalem is portrayed as ruined and deserted (44:26; 58:12), and the people are portrayed as suffering at the hands of the Chaldeans (42:22, 25; 47:6).

Those whom the writer is addressing are not the contemporaries of Isaiah in Jerusalem, but those in Babylon. Since the prophets, they contend, always spoke to their contemporaries, this rules out ascribing the authorship to Isaiah.

The literary style of chapters 40–66 purportedly is completely different from 1–39, containing many words and expressions which are not used in the earlier part of the book. The style of 1–39 is said to be majestic and solemn, while 40–66 supposedly is more personal, passionate, and dramatic.

It is argued that the theology of Second Isaiah is different from 1–39, with Isaiah emphasizing God's dignity and power, while 40–66 depicts His quality of infinity. Deutero-Isaiah speaks of the servant of the Lord, while chapters 1–39 describe the kingly Messiah.

It is also argued that the name of Isaiah is nowhere mentioned in 40–66, and that Cyrus is named 150 years before his time (44:28; 45:1), if the second portion is ascribed to Isaiah.

The above arguments are inconclusive for the following reasons:

The standpoint of chapters 40–66 does indeed presuppose the exile, but the writer is speaking from an ideal—not an actual—point of view. Isaiah intentionally speaks and thinks in this future period, as if it were the present.

Examples of this same thing can be found in Ezekiel 40–48, Nahum 2, 3 and the entire Book of Revelation. It is simply not true that a prophet always speaks only to the needs of his own contemporaries (Zechariah 9–14; Daniel 11, 12). Isaiah is projected into the future to foretell the promised deliverance from captivity.

The difference in style between 1–39 and 40–66 is not as pronounced as the critical school likes to believe. The change in subject matter accounts for this difference, and any argument of the kind the critics use is very subjective and inconclusive.

Moreover, the similarities in style are not sufficiently considered by the critics. The phrase, "the holy one of Israel," occurs more than a dozen times in each section, but is rarely used in the rest of the Old Testament. Many passages show actual verbal agreement or such similarity in thought and metaphor that the unity of the two sections is demonstrated.

The so-called theological differences are non-existent, since the elevated ideas of God in 40–66 are easily explained by the subject matter.

Isaiah's name does appear at the head of the book (1:1), which clearly applies to all 66 chapters. If chapters 40–66 had Isaiah's name, no doubt the critical school would have rejected this as a later addition inserted by an editor.

There is absolutely no manuscript or historical evidence that the entire 66 chapters were written by anyone other than the one Isaiah. The Isaiah scroll, from the Dead Sea Scrolls, dates from the second century before Christ, with chapter 40 beginning on the last line of the column, which contains chapters 38:8–40:2. This is a strong early witness to the unity of Isaiah.

The mention of Cyrus by name a century and a half before his time is no problem for those who believe in predictive prophecy. The same thing can be found in the foretelling of Josiah's name and reign three centuries before his birth (I Kings 13:1, 2) and the prophecy of the birthplace of Christ (Micah 5:2) 700 years before it occurred.

The concluding point in advocating the unity of Isaiah is the witness of the New Testament. Isaiah is quoted by name twenty-one times in the New Testament from both sections of the book. John 12:38–40 contains two quotations from both sections of Isaiah (53:1; 6:9), and John 12:41 (KJV) says, "These things said Isaiah." Jesus read from Isaiah 61:1, which according to Luke 4:17 (KJV) was "the book of the prophet Isaiah."

One other line ignored by liberal critics is the authors reference to the flora and climate of the book. In no way do the flora, climate or geography in Isaiah 40 to 66 fit with out knowledge of Babylon, yet they show great familiarity to Palestine where the book purports to have been written.

Thus it seems safe to conclude that all 66 chapters were written by the prophet Isaiah ca. 739–680 B.C.

✚ ADDITIONAL REFERENCE SOURCES

Gleason Archer, *A Survey of Old Testament Introduction*, rev. ed., Moody Press, 1979

E. J. Young, *Who Wrote Isaiah?* Eerdmans, 1958

Hobart Freeman, *An Introduction to the Old Testament Prophets,* Moody Press, 1968

 **I've heard each of you say that the existence of the Jewish people today is objective evidence that the Bible is true. Why?**

If anyone wishes to know whether or not the God of the Bible exists, one of the strongest reasons he can examine is the Jewish people. An honest inquiry into this question will provide more than an adequate answer to the truthfulness of the Christian faith.

About 4,000 years ago, God called a man named Abram out of the country where he was living and gave him these promises, "I will make you a great nation, and I will bless you, and make your name great; and so you shall be a blessing; and I will bless those that bless you, and the one who curses you I will curse. And in you all the families of the earth shall be blessed" (Genesis 12:2, 3, NASB).

"And the Lord said to Abram . . . Now lift up your eyes and look from the place where you are, northward and southward and eastward and westward; for all the land which you see, I will give it to you and to your descendants forever" (Genesis 13:14, 15, NASB).

In other words, God promised to Abram (1) a great nation; (2) a great name; (3) being a blessing to all nations; and (4) a land which shall forever belong to his descendants.

Several hundred years after God made these promises to Abram, the great nation had indeed appeared, numbering in the millions. They were about to enter the land of promise when God, through their leader, Moses, gave them some warnings as recorded in Deuteronomy chapters 28-33.

God warned them against disobedience and promised that He would use other nations to remove them from that land if they were unfaithful to Him. He predicted that they would eventually be scattered across the whole earth as strangers in unfamiliar lands and that they would find no rest from their wanderings. However, God in His faithfulness did promise to bring them back into their land.

What has been the verdict of history? The children of Israel, even though they were warned, fell into idolatry and were removed from their homeland. In 606 B.C. King Nebuchadnezzar took the people captive to Babylon and returned in 588–586 B.C., and after a long siege burned the city and the temple.

However, as God promised, He allowed those who desired to return to the land in 537–536 B.C. or after seventy years (Ezra, chapter 1). The removal from their homeland occurred a second time in A.D. 70 when Titus the Roman destroyed the city of Jerusalem and scattered the people.

For almost 1,900 years, the Jews wandered about the earth as strangers who were persecuted from every side. This culminated in the holocaust of World War II, when six million Jews were put to death in the concentration camps.

Yet, against all odds, the state of Israel was reborn on May 14, 1948, and the Jews began to return to their homeland from all points of the compass. This was the second time in their history since becoming a nation that they have come back into their land. Since 1948 they have survived some terrible conflicts, including the 1967 Six-Day War and the 1973 Holy Day War.

Through all this, the nation neither perished nor lost its national identity. History has demonstrated that any people who leave their homeland will, after about five generations, lose their national identity by being absorbed into the new culture, but the Jews remained a distinct entity.

Not only have they survived, but the nations that persecuted them—Moab, Ammon, Edom, Philistia, and many others—have either been destroyed or completely lost their individual identity.

Have you ever heard of a Swedish Moabite? A Russian Philistine? A German Edomite? An American Ammonite? No! These people have been totally absorbed into other cultures and races.

However, have you ever heard of a Swedish Jew? A Russian Jew? A German Jew? An American Jew? Yes! As prophesied, they have not lost their identity.

One of us was once attending a debate over the person of Jesus Christ in which a rabbi was participating. During the question period, the rabbi was asked why he did not believe in the resurrection of Jesus. "I don't believe in the miracles of the New Testament," he replied.

Some sharp student immediately asked the rabbi why he rejected the New Testament miracles but accepted the Old Testament miracles, and on what basis he made the distinction. Without batting an eye, the rabbi replied, "That's easy; I don't believe in the Old Testament miracles either. I think they are all myths." It's hard to believe he could make a statement like that, considering the fact that his survival, as a Jew, is one of the greatest miracles in all history.

When the two of us were in Israel in 1976, filming the movie, "More Than a Carpenter," we were invited to meet with a high official of the Israeli government. One of the questions we asked him concerned the survival of his nation.

How did they manage to survive being twice removed from their homeland, the second time almost 1,900 years; survive the holocaust when one out of every three Jews living was put to death, and stave off the attacks of the more than 100 million members of the Arab world in both 1967 and 1973?

Was this a result of their nation being so resourceful or was it because some divine hand was watching over His people? He looked up at the two of us and said, "Although most of the people in my country today would claim to be atheists, don't you believe it. I think that all of us know deep down inside that some force greater than us has been protecting this nation."

He added that after the recent recapturing of Jerusalem by the Jews, there were at one time about a million people either at or on their way to the wailing wall to give thanks to God.

The God of the Bible is faithful. He has demonstrated both His existence and faithfulness by His dealing with national Israel as an objective sign to the world, testifying to His existence and verifying His promises.

✚ ADDITIONAL REFERENCE SOURCES

Josh McDowell, "The 7-Point Whammy" (tape), Liberation Tapes, P.O. Box 6044, Lubbock, Texas 79413

Don Stewart, "Reasons Why I Believe" (tape), The Word for Today, P.O. Box 8000, Costa Mesa, Calif. 92626

Why do I always hear Christians appealing to fulfilled prophecy to prove the inspiration of the Bible?

Believers in Jesus Christ are constantly being asked why they believe the Bible to be inspired, and a common response is because of fulfilled prophecy. The argument from fulfilled prophecy is one of the strongest imaginable.

The apostle Peter, after testifying that he had seen Jesus Christ in all His glory, said, "And so we have the prophetic word made more sure, to which you do well to pay attention as to a lamp shining in a dark place, until the day dawns and the morning star arises in your hearts" (II Peter 1:19, NASB). Peter here is appealing to fulfilled prophecy as a witness to the truth of the Scriptures.

The Bible itself gives the purpose of prophecy, "Remember the former things long past, for I am God, and there is no other; I am God, and there is no one like Me, declaring the end from the beginning and from ancient times things which have not been done . . ." (Isaiah 46:9, 10, NASB).

"I declared the former things long ago and they went forth from My mouth, and I proclaimed them. Suddenly I acted, and they came to pass. . . . Therefore I declared them to you long ago, before they took place I proclaimed them to you, lest you should say, 'My idol has done them, and my graven image and my molten image have commanded them'" (Isaiah 48:3, 5, NASB).

The New Testament spoke of the coming of Jesus Christ, "Which he promised beforehand through his prophets in the holy scriptures" (Romans 1:1–4, RSV).

The testimony of the Scriptures is that the purpose of prophecy is to let us know that God exists and that He has a plan for this world. By the foretelling of persons, places, and events hundreds of years before their occurrence, the Bible demonstrates a knowledge of the future that is too specific to be labeled a good guess. By giving examples of fulfilled prophecy, the Scriptures give a strong testimony to their own inspiration.

An example of this would be the prophecy of King Cyrus (Isaiah 44:28; 45:1). The prophet Isaiah, writing about 700 B.C., predicts Cyrus by name as the king who will say to Jerusalem that it shall be built and that the temple foundation shall be laid.

At the time of Isaiah's writing, the city of Jerusalem was fully built and the entire temple was standing. Not until more than 100 years later would the city and temple be destroyed by King Nebuchadnezzar in 586 B.C.

After Jerusalem was taken by the Babylonians, it was conquered by the Persians in about 539 B.C. Shortly after that, a Persian king named Cyrus gave the decree to rebuild the temple in Jerusalem. This was around 160 years after the prophecy of Isaiah!

Thus Isaiah predicted that a man named Cyrus, who would not be born for about 100 years, would give the command to rebuild the temple which was still standing in Isaiah's day and would not be destroyed for more than 100 years. This prophecy is truly amazing, but it is not isolated.

There are, in fact, literally hundreds of prophecies which predict future events. The idea that the fulfillment of the predictions is a result of coincidence or chance is absurd, in light of the evidence. God has given sufficient evidence of His existence and of the divine inspiration of the Scriptures by means of fulfilled prophecy.

✚ ADDITIONAL REFERENCE SOURCES

Peter Stoner, *Science Speaks*, Moody Press, 1958

Josh McDowell, *Evidence That Demands a Verdict*, vol. 1, ch. 9, rev. ed., Here's Life Publishers, 1979

What is the apocrypha? Why aren't these books found in Protestant Bibles?

Today the word apocrypha is synonymous with the fourteen or fifteen books of doubtful authenticity and authority. These writings are not found in the Hebrew Old Testament, but they are contained in some manuscripts of the Septuagint, the Greek translation of the Hebrew Old Testament, which was completed around 250 B.C. in Alexandria, Egypt.

Most of these books were declared to be Scripture by the Roman Catholic Church at the Council of Trent (1545–1563), though the Protestant Church rejects any divine authority attached to them.

Those who attribute divine authority to these books and advocate them as Scripture argue that the writers of the New Testament quote mostly from the Septuagint, which contains the apocrypha. They also cite the fact that some of the Church fathers, notably Iranaeus, Tertullian, and Clement of Alexandria, used the apocrypha in public worship and accepted them as Scripture, as did the Syriac Church in the fourth century.

St. Augustine, who presided over the councils at Hippo and Carthage, concurred with their decision that the books of the apocrypha were inspired. The Greek Church adds its weight to the list of believers in the inspiration of the apocrypha.

The advocates point also to the Dead Sea Scrolls to add further weight to their belief in the apocrypha. Among the fragments at Qumran are copies of some of the apocryphal books written in Hebrew. These have been discovered alongside other Old Testament works.

The case for including the apocrypha as holy Scripture completely breaks down when examined. The New Testament writers may allude to the apocrypha, but they *never* quote from it as holy Scripture or give the slightest hint that any of the books are inspired. If the Septuagint in the first century contained these books, which is by no means a proven fact, Jesus and His disciples completely ignored them.

Appealing to certain Church fathers as proof of the inspiration of the books is a weak argument, since just as many in the early church, notably Origen, Jerome, and others, denied their alleged inspiration.

The Syriac Church waited until the fourth century A.D. to accept these books as canonical. It is notable that the Peshitta, the Syriac Bible of the second century A.D., did not contain them.

The early Augustine did acknowledge the apocrypha, at least in part. But later, Augustine's writings clearly reflected a rejection of these books as outside the canon and inferior to the Hebrew scriptures.

The Jewish community also rejected these writings. At the Jewish Council of Jamnia (c. A.D. 90), nine of the books of our Old Testament canon were debated for differing reasons whether they were to be included. Eventually they ruled that only the Hebrew Old Testament books of our present canon were canonical.

Citing the presence of the apocrypha among the Old Testament fragments proves little regarding inspiration, as numerous fragments of other, non-Scriptural documents were also found.

It cannot be overemphasized that the Roman Catholic church itself did not officially declare these books Holy Scripture until 1545-1563 at the Council of Trent.

The acceptance of certain books in the apocrypha as canonical by the Roman Catholic church was to a great extent a reaction to the Protestant Reformation. By canonizing these books, they legitimized their reference to them in doctrinal matters.

The arguments that advocate the scriptural authority of the apocrypha obviously leave a great deal to be desired.

There are some other telling reasons why the apocrypha is rejected by the Protestant church. One of these deals with the unbiblical teaching of these questionable books, such as praying for the dead.

Praying for the deceased, advocated in II Maccabees 12:45–46, is in direct opposition to Luke 16:25, 26 and Hebrews 9:27, among others. The apocrypha also contains the episode which has God assisting Judith in a lie (Judith 9:10, 13).

The apocrypha contains demonstrable errors as well. Tobit was supposedly alive when Jeroboam staged his revolt in 931 B.C. and was still living at the time of the Assyrian captivity (722 B.C.), yet the Book of Tobit says he lived only 158 years (Tobit 1:3-5; 14:11).

Finally, there is no claim in any of these apocryphal books as to divine inspiration. One need only read these works alongside the Bible to see the vast difference.

✚ ADDITIONAL REFERENCE SOURCES

Norman Geisler and William Nix, *A General Introduction to the Bible*, Moody Press, 1973

Merrill Unger, *Unger's Bible Dictionary*, rev. ed., Chicago, Moody Press, 1971

G. Douglas Young, "The Apocrypha" in *Revelation and the Bible,* edited by Carl Henry, Baker Book House

Bruce M. Metzger, *An Introduction to the Apocrypha*, Oxford Univ. Press, 1957

 **Did Jesus claim to be God? Even if He did make the claim, why should I believe it?**

Among the religious leaders who have attained a large following throughout history, Jesus Christ is unique in the fact that He alone claimed to be God in human flesh. A common misconception is that some or many of the leaders of the world's religions made similar claims, but this is simply not the case.

Buddha did not claim to be God; Moses never said that he was Yahweh; Mohammed did not identify himself as Allah; and nowhere will you find Zoroaster claiming to be Ahura Mazda. Yet Jesus, the carpenter from Nazareth, said that he who has seen Him (Jesus) has seen the Father (John 14:9).

The claims of Christ are many and varied. He said that He existed before Abraham (John 8:58), and that He was equal with the Father (John 5:17, 18). Jesus claimed the ability to forgive sins (Mark 2:5–7), which the Bible teaches was something that God alone could do (Isaiah 43:25).

The New Testament equated Jesus as the creator of the universe (John 1:3), and that He is the one who holds everything together (Colossians 1:17). The apostle Paul says that God was manifest in the flesh (I Timothy 3:16, KJV), and John the evangelist says that "the Word was God" (John 1:1). The united testimony of Jesus and the writers of the New Testament is that He was more than mere man; He *was* God.

Not only did His friends notice that He claimed to be God, but so did His enemies as well. There may be some doubt today among the skeptics who refuse to examine the evidence, but there was no doubt on the part of the Jewish authorities.

When Jesus asked them why they wanted to stone Him, they replied, "For a good work we do not stone You, but for blasphemy; and because You, being a man, make Yourself out to be God" (John 10:33, NASB).

This fact separates Jesus from the other religious figures. In the major religions of the world, the teachings—not the teacher—are all-important.

Confucianism is a set of teachings; Confucius is not important. Islam is the revelation of Allah, with Mohammed being the prophet, and Buddhism emphasizes the principles of the Buddha and not Buddha himself. This is especially true of Hinduism, where there is no historic founder.

However, at the center of Christianity is the person of Jesus Christ. Jesus did not just claim to be teaching mankind the truth; He claimed that *He* was the truth (John 14:6).

What Jesus taught is not the important aspect of Christianity, but what is important is *who* Jesus was. Was He the Son of God? Is He the only way a person can reach God? This was the claim He made for Himself.

Suppose this very night the President of the United States appeared on all the major networks and proclaimed that "I am God Almighty. I have the power to forgive sin. I have the authority to raise my life back from the dead."

He would be quickly and quietly shut off the air, led away, and replaced by the Vice-President. Anybody who would dare make such claims would have to be either out of his mind or a liar, unless he was God.

This is exactly the case with Jesus. He clearly claimed all these things and more. If He is God, as He claimed, we must believe in Him, and if He is not, then we should have nothing to do with Him. Jesus is either Lord of all or not Lord at all.

Yes, Jesus claimed to be God. Why should anyone believe it? After all, merely claiming to be something does not make it true. Where's the evidence that Jesus is God?

The Bible gives various reasons, including miracles and fulfilled prophecy, that are intended to convince us that Jesus is the one whom He said He was (John 20:30, 31). The main reason, or the sign which Jesus Himself said would demonstrate that He was the Son of God, was His resurrection from the dead.

When asked for a sign from the religious leaders, Jesus replied, "For as Jonah was three days and three nights in the belly of the whale, so will the Son of man be three days and three nights in the heart of the earth" (Matthew 12:40, RSV).

In another place He said, when asked for a sign, "Destroy this temple, and in three days I will raise it up . . . but he spake of the temple of his body" (John 2:19, 21, KJV). The ability to raise His life back from the dead was the sign that separates Him not only from all other religious leaders, but also from anyone else who has ever lived.

Anyone wishing to refute the case for Christianity must explain away the story of the resurrection. Therefore, according to the Bible, Jesus proves to be the Son of God by coming back from the dead (Romans 1:4). The evidence is overwhelming that Jesus did rise from the grave, and it is this fact that proves Jesus to be God.

✚ ADDITIONAL REFERENCE SOURCES

Josh McDowell, *Evidence That Demands a Verdict*, rev. ed., Here's Life Publishers, 1979

Josh McDowell, *More Than a Carpenter*, Tyndale House, 1977

Arlie J. Hoover, *Dear Agnos*, Baker Book House, 1976

Michael Green (ed.), *The Truth of God Incarnate*, Eerdmans, 1977

Sir Norman Anderson, *Mystery of the Incarnation*, Inter-Varsity Press, 1978

A friend of mine said Jesus never existed. How do you answer something like this?

There are still many people today who make the claim that Jesus never existed, that He was only a mythical character.

Bertrand Russell puts it this way, "I may say that one is not concerned with the historical question. Historically, it is quite doubtful whether Christ ever existed at all, and if He did we do not know anything about Him, so I am not concerned with the historical question, which is a very difficult one. I am concerned with Christ as He appears in the Gospels" (*Why I Am Not a Christian*, p. 11, note 8).

However, those who make such an accusation are certainly not historians, but are surprisingly ignorant of the facts.

The New Testament contains twenty-seven separate documents which were written in the first century A.D. These writings contain the story of the life of Jesus and the beginnings of the Christian church from about 4 B.C. until the decade of the A.D. nineties.

The facts were recorded by eyewitnesses, who gave first-hand testimony to what they had seen and heard. "What was from the beginning, what we have heard, what we have seen with our eyes, what we beheld and our hands handled, concerning the Word of Life" (I John 1:1, NASB).

Moreover, the existence of Jesus is recorded by the Jewish historian, Flavius Josephus, who was born in A.D. 37, "Now there was about this time, Jesus, a wise man, if it be lawful to call him a man, for he was a doer of wonderful works—a teacher of such men as receive the truth with pleasure. He drew over to him both many of the Jews, and many of the Gentiles.

"He was (the) Christ; and when Pilate, at the suggestion of the principal men amongst us, had condemned him to the cross, those who loved him at the firs did not forsake him, for he appeared to them alive again the third day, as the divine prophets had foretold these and ten thousand other wonderful things concerning him; and the tribe of Christians, so named from him, are not extinct at this day" (*Antiquities*, XVIII, III).

Although this passage has been contested because of the reference to Jesus being the Christ and rising from the dead, the fact of His existence is not in question.

Cornelius Tacitus (A.D. 112), a Roman historian, writing about the reign of Nero, refers to Jesus Christ and the existence of Christians in Rome (*Annals*, XV, 44). Tacitus, elsewhere in his *Histories*, refers to Christianity when alluding to the burning of the temple of Jerusalem in A.D. 70. This has been preserved by Sulpicius Severus (Chronicles 30:6).

There are other references to Jesus or His followers, such as the Roman historian, Seutonius (A.D. 120) in *Life of Claudius*, 25.4, and *Lives of the Caesars*, 26.2, and Pliny the younger (A.D. 112) in his *Epistles*, X. 96.

This testimony, both Christian and non-Christian, is more than sufficient to lay to rest any idea that Jesus, in fact, never existed. In light of the evidence, it is absurd to hold such a view. We know more about the life of Jesus than just about any other figure in the ancient world. His birth, life, and death are revealed in much more detail than most ancient figures whose existence is taken for granted by historians.

After examining the evidence about the life of Christ from contemporary sources apart from the New Testament, Roderic Dunkerley concluded, "In none of these various testimonies to the fact of Christ is there any slightest hint or idea that he was not a real historical person.

"Indeed it has been argued—and I think very rightly—that myth theories of the beginnings of Christianity are modern speculative hypotheses motivated by unreasoning prejudice and dislike. 'It would never enter anyone's head,' says Merezhovsky, to ask whether Jesus had lived, unless before asking the question the mind had been darkened by the wish that he had not lived'" (Roderic Dunkerley, *Beyond the Gospels*, pp. 29, 30).

✚ ADDITIONAL REFERENCE SOURCES

F. F. Bruce, *The New Testament Documents: Are They Reliable?*, rev. ed., Eerdmans, 1977

Josh McDowell, *Evidence That Demands a Verdict*, rev. ed., Here's Life Publishers, 1979

John Warwick Montgomery, *History and Christianity*, Here's Life Publishers, 1983

Q Don't the Gospels give contradictory reports as to the time Christ was crucified?

A One of the so-called contradictions that we hear brought up concerns the disagreement between the Gospel of Mark and the Gospel of John as to the time of the crucifixion of Jesus.

Mark 15:25 (KJV) states, "and it was the third hour, and they crucified him," while in John 19:14 (KJV) we read, "And it was the preparation of the passover, and about the sixth hour: and he saith unto the Jews, Behold your King!"

This does indeed present a difficulty, since Mark has Jesus being crucified at the third hour, or nine o'clock in the morning, according to Jewish reckoning, while John places Jesus before Pontius Pilate at about the sixth hour, or noon.

Many say this discrepancy is impossible to reconcile, while others say the difference between the two is a result of a mistake early in the copying process. Neither of these two views is plausible or acceptable.

There are two possible solutions which carry reasonable weight. One solution centers on the word "about" in John's statement of the time. He reveals that it was not exactly the sixth hour, but only *about* this time.

Also, Mark's account does not force us to believe that it was at exactly 9 a.m. when Jesus was put on the cross. This can be observed by understanding the way the New Testament calculates time.

The night was divided into four watches, each consisting of three hours (see Mark 13:35), and the day was to some extent likewise divided into periods. In light of this, we can imagine that Mark's statement about the "third hour" simply meant that Jesus was crucified sometime during the third hour (between nine o'clock and noon), while John's statement that the trial ended *about* noon can mean before noon.

Thus, if the crucifixion took place between nine o'clock and noon, Mark could have placed it at the earlier period (nine o'clock) and John at the later period (noon) without there being any discrepancy.

"If the crucifixion took place midway between nine and twelve o'clock, it was quite natural that one observer should refer it to the former, while another referred it to the latter hour.

"The height of the sun in the sky was the index of the time of the day; while it was easy to know whether it was before or after midday, or whether the sun was more or less than halfway between the zenith and the horizon, finer distinctions of time were not recognized without consulting the sun dials, which were not everywhere at hand" (*The Expositor's Greek New Testament*, commenting on John 19:14).

Another possibility is that John is using a different method of reckoning time than Mark. We know for a fact, from Plutarch, Pliny, Aulus Gellius, and Macrobius, that the Romans calculated the civil day from midnight to midnight, just as we do today.

Thus John's "sixth hour" would be six o'clock in the morning. This would make 6 a.m. the time of the last of the trials of Jesus, and of His sentencing, giving adequate time for the events leading up to the crucifixion which, in Mark, was at 9 a.m. or afterward.

There is good evidence that John used this method of computing time. This is not unusual in Scripture to have different authors use different methods of measuring time and determining dates.

In the Old Testament, the writers often would state their important dates by the calendar system of the country they were serving under at that time. For instance, in Jeremiah 25:1 and 46:2, the time was by Palestinian reckoning, and Daniel 1:1 was Babylonian reckoning, the same year.

A New Testament example is John 20:19. The evening of the day Jesus rose from the dead is considered part of that same day. Apparently John is not reckoning by Jewish time. According to the Jewish system of reckoning time, the evening in question would be part of Monday, the first day of the week, since the Jewish day began at sunset.

This possible factor, along with the one previously mentioned, shows that the difficulty in these two passages is not at all impossible to solve, nor does it pose any difficulty that is without a reasonable explanation.

✚ ADDITIONAL REFERENCE SOURCES

W.F. Arndt, *Does the Bible Contradict Itself?*, 5th rev. ed., Concordia Press, 1955

The Expositor's Greek Testament, Edited by W. Robertson Nicoll, Eerdmans, 1951

How do we know that Jesus rose from the dead?

Did Jesus actually rise from the dead? Does it really matter whether He did or didn't?

Ronald Gregor Smith gives a typical reply, "So far as historicity is concerned . . . it is necessary to explain: We may freely say that the bones of Jesus lie somewhere in Palestine. Christian faith is not destroyed by this admission.

"On the contrary, only now, when this has been said, are we in a position to ask about the meaning of the resurrection as an integral part of the message concerning Jesus" (*Secular Christianity*, London, Collins, 1966, p. 103).

Contrary to this point of view, it does matter to Christianity whether or not it is true that Christ came back from the dead, because Christianity stands or falls on the resurrection of Jesus Christ (I Corinthians 15:12–19). If Jesus did not come back from the dead, then the Christian faith crumbles.

Fortunately, one of the most well-attested events in the ancient world is the resurrection of Jesus Christ from the dead. When confronted by the religious leaders of His day, Jesus was asked for a sign to demonstrate that He was the promised Messiah.

He answered, "An evil and adulterous generation craves for a sign; and yet no sign shall be given to it but the sign of Jonah the prophet; for just as Jonah was three days and three nights in the belly of the sea monster, so shall the Son of Man be three days and three nights in the heart of the earth" (Matthew 12:39, 40, NASB).

The sign of the resurrection was meant to set Jesus apart from anyone else who ever lived, and it would designate Him the Son of God (Romans 1:4).

The accounts of His appearances are recorded for us by eyewitnesses to whom Jesus appeared alive over a forty-day period after His public crucifixion. As the scriptural account sets forth, to these "he shewed himself alive after his passion by many infallible proofs, being seen of them forty days, and speaking of the things pertaining to the kingdom of God" (Acts 1:3, KJV).

Writing about A.D. 56, the apostle Paul mentions the fact that more than 500 people had witnessed the resurrected Christ at one time and most of them were still living when he wrote (I Corinthians 15:6). This statement is somewhat of a challenge to those who might not have believed, since Paul is saying that there are many people yet living who could be interviewed to find out if Christ had indeed risen.

The historical evidence is more than sufficient to satisfy the curiosity of the honest inquirer. This can be seen not only by the positive defense that can be made for the case for the resurrection, but also by the lack of any evidence for an alternative explanation. The theories attempting to give an alternative explanation to the resurrection take more faith to believe than the resurrection itself.

Frank Morrison, who was an agnostic journalist, attempted to write a book refuting the resurrection of Christ. After much investigation, his opinion changed and he became a believer in Jesus Christ. This is how Morrison described what happened to him:

"This study is in some ways so unusual and provocative that the writer thinks it desirable to state here very briefly how the book came to take its present form. In one sense it could have taken no other, for it is essentially a confession, the inner story of a man who originally set out to write one kind of book and found himself compelled by the sheer force of circumstances to write another.

"It is not that the facts altered, for they are recorded imperishably in the monuments and in the pages of human history. But the interpretation to be put on the facts underwent a change" (*Who Moved the Stone?* Preface, Zondervan, 1971).

Morrison discovered that Christ was publicly put in the tomb on Friday, but on Sunday morning the body was missing. If He did not rise from the dead, then someone took the body.

There are three interest groups that could possibly have taken the body: the Romans, the Jews, or the disciples.

The Romans would have had no reason to steal the body, since they wanted to keep the peace in Palestine. The idea was to keep the provinces as quiet as possible, and stealing the body of Christ would not accomplish this objective.

The Jews would not have taken the body, because the last thing they wanted was a proclamation of the resurrection. They are the ones who asked for the guard, according to Matthew 27.

The disciples of Jesus had no reason to steal the body, and if they did, they later died for something they knew to be untrue. Moreover, the religion which they proclaimed emphasized telling the truth and not lying. Their actions would have been inconsistent with that which they knew to be true and commanded others to follow.

The other reasonable explanation is that Christ has risen, and the eyewitnesses make it plain this is the case. The disciples of Jesus may not have been as sophisticated as twentieth century man in the realm of scientific knowledge, but they surely knew the difference between someone who was dead and someone who wasn't.

As Simon Peter said, "For we did not follow cleverly devised tales when we made known to you the power and coming of our Lord Jesus Christ, but we were eyewitnesses of His majesty" (II Peter 1:16, NASB).

✚ ADDITIONAL REFERENCE SOURCES

Frank Morrison, *Who Moved the Stone?*, Zondervan, 1971

George Ladd, *I Believe in the Resurrection of Jesus*, Grand Rapids, Eerdmans, 1975

Josh McDowell, "The Great Resurrection Hoax" (tape), Liberation Tapes, P.O. Box 6044, Lubbock, Texas 79413

Don Stewart, "The Resurrection: The Cornerstone of Christianity" (tape), The Word for Today, P.O. Box 8000, Costa Mesa, Calif. 92626

Josh McDowell, *Evidence That Demands a Verdict*, Vol. 1, rev. ed., 1979 p. 179–263

**How could Jesus have remained in the tomb three days and three nights if He was crucified on Friday and rose on Sunday?**

Jesus prophesied in Matthew 12:40 (NASB) that "just as Jonah was three days and three nights in the belly of the sea monster, so shall the Son of Man be three days and three nights in the heart of the earth."

The accounts of His death and resurrection as given in the Gospels of Matthew, Mark, Luke, and John indicate that Jesus was crucified and buried on Friday, before sundown, which is the beginning of the next day for the Jews, and resurrected on the first day of the week, which is our Sunday, before sunrise.

This puts Jesus in the grave for part of Friday, the entire Sabbath, and part of Sunday. In other words, two full nights, one full day and part of two days, He was in the tomb. Since this is clearly not three full, twenty-four-hour days, do we have a problem of conflict with the prophecy of Jesus in Matthew 12:40?

In Mark 8:31 and Matthew 16:21, Jesus is recorded as saying, "The Son of man will rise again after three days," and "He will be raised again on the third day"—expressions that are used interchangeably. This can be seen from the fact that the most references to the resurrection state that it occurred *on* the third day.

Also, Jesus, in addition to the Matthew 12:40 passage, spoke of His resurrection in John 2:19–22, stating that He would be raised up *in* three days (not the fourth day).

Matthew 27:63 (KJV) gives weight to this idiomatic usage. After the Pharisees tell Pilate of the prediction of Jesus, "After three days I will rise again," they ask for a guard to secure the tomb until the third day.

If the phrase, "after three days," was not interchangeable with the "third day," the Pharisees would have asked for a guard for the fourth day.

That the expression "one day and one night" was an idiom employed by the Jews for indicating a day, even when only a part of a day was indicated, can be seen also in the Old Testament.

For example, I Samuel 30:12, 13 (KJV), "For he had not eaten bread or drunk water for three days and three nights," and in the next verse, "My master left me behind . . . three days ago."

Just as clearly, Genesis 42:17 shows this idiomatic usage. Joseph imprisoned his brothers for three days; in verse 18, he speaks to them and releases them, all on the third day.

The phrases, "after three days" and "on the third day," are not contradictory, either to each other or with Matthew 12:40, but simply idiomatic, interchangeable terms, clearly a common mode of Jewish expression.

✚ ADDITIONAL REFERENCE SOURCES

Harold Hoehner, *Chronological Aspects of the Life of Christ*, Zondervan, 1977

W.F. Arndt, *Does the Bible Contradict Itself?*, 5th rev. ed., Concordia Press, 1955

How do you explain the contradictions in the resurrection story?

The New Testament makes the assertion that the truth of Christianity stands or falls on the resurrection of Jesus.

The apostle Paul stated, "If Christ be not risen, then is our preaching vain, and your faith is also vain. Yea, and we are found false witnesses of God; because we have testified of God that he raised up Christ. . . . And if Christ be not raised, your faith is vain; ye are yet in your sins . . . . If in this life only we have hope in Christ, we are of all men most miserable" (I Corinthians 15:14, 15, 17, 19, KJV).

A common objection to the fact of the resurrection is that the four Gospel narratives contain hopeless contradictions. If the four accounts were placed in parallel columns, a number of apparent differences would be highlighted. However, these apparent differences ultimately confirm the truthfulness of these accounts, rather than refute them.

If all four Gospels gave exactly the same story, in exactly the same order, with exactly the same details, we would immediately become suspicious. We could also wonder why all four writers did not simply attach their names as co-authors of *one* account. Obviously, this is not the case. None of the four Gospels gives all the details of what transpired.

Matthew is the only writer who records the first appearance to the women, while only in Luke do we find the account of the two disciples on the road to Emmaus. The appearance of Mary Magdalene is omitted by both Matthew and Luke. Only John records the appearance of our Lord in the upper room, when Thomas was absent and the appearance on the sea of Galilee.

It is quite clear that all of the Gospels relate their portraits of Jesus differently. This is what we should expect. No four witnesses (or news reporters), all of whom witness a series of events, will write them up in exactly the same way, detail for detail. If they did, there would be obvious collusion.

If the differences concerned the main points of the story, then there would be justification for doubt, but when the salient points are agreed upon by every witness, insignificant differences add to, rather than subtract from, the validity.

It should be noted, too, that none of the details necessarily flatly contradicts any others, but in some plausible way they correlate together to supply the larger picture. The variations in detail the different writers chose to include in the resurrection narratives consist of incidental things which in no way jeopardize the main plot of the story.

One of the seeming contradictions that bothers people concerns the time the women came to the tomb, related differently by John and Mark. Mark's account has the women coming to the tomb at the rising of the sun, while John states that Mary Magdalene came to the tomb when it was dark.

This difficulty is solved when it is realized that the women had to walk quite some distance to reach the grave, since they stayed in Jerusalem or Bethany. It was dark when they left the place in which they were staying, but when they arrived at the tomb the sun was beginning to shine. Therefore, Mark is speaking of their arrival, while John refers to their departure.

The area which has generated the most discussion concerns the angels who were at the tomb of Jesus. Matthew and Mark relate that one angel addressed the women, while Luke and John say that two angels were at the tomb.

This seems to be a discrepancy, with Matthew and Mark knowing of only one angel while Luke and John speak of two. However, Matthew and Mark do not say that there was *only* one angel at the tomb, but that one angel spoke to the women.

This does not contradict Luke and John, for Matthew and Mark specify that one angel spoke, but they do not say there was only one angel present or only one angel spoke. Quite possibly one of the angels served as the spokesman for the two, thus he was emphasized. There is no need to assume a discrepancy.

Though they report some of the details differently, the Gospels agree in all important points. The accounts are in harmony on the fact that Jesus was dead and buried; that the disciples were not prepared for His death, but were totally confused; that the tomb was empty on Easter morning; that the empty tomb did not convince them that Jesus had risen; that Mary thought the body had been stolen.

The Gospel writers also concur that the disciples had certain experiences which they believed to be appearances of the resurrected Christ. That normative first century Judaism had no concept of a dying and rising Messiah is a historical fact.

The disciples proclaimed the resurrection story in Jerusalem, in the place where Jesus had been killed and buried. All these facts considered together constitute a powerful argument for the validity of the resurrection story.

The venerable scholar, Wilbur Smith, had this to say about the differences in the resurrection accounts and the areas in which the Gospels agree:

"In these fundamental truths, there are absolutely no contradictions. The so-called variations in the narratives are only the details which were mostly vividly impressed on one mind or another of the witnesses of our Lord's resurrection, or on the mind of the writers of these four respective Gospels.

"The closest, most critical, examination of these narratives throughout the ages never has destroyed and can never destroy their powerful testimony to the truth that Christ did rise from the dead on the third day, and was seen of many" (*The Supernaturalness of Christ*, W.A. Wilde Company, 1954, p. 205).

✚ ADDITIONAL REFERENCE SOURCES

George Ladd, *I Believe in the Resurrection of Jesus*, Eerdmans, 1975

Wilbur Smith, *The Supernaturalness of Christ*, W.A. Wilde Company, 1954

W.J. Sparrow-Simpson, *The Resurrection and the Christian Faith*, Zondervan, 1968

Merrill Tenney, *The Reality of the Resurrection*, Harper and Row, 1963

Do you believe Jesus was born of a virgin?

A The miracle of the virgin birth of Jesus Christ has perplexed many people and has actually kept them from accepting the truth of Christianity. However, the Bible declares that God decided that His Son would have a miraculous entrance into humanity.

Seven hundred years before the birth of Christ, the prophet Isaiah said, "Therefore the Lord Himself will give you a sign: Behold, a virgin will be with child and bear a son, and she will call His name Immanuel" (Isaiah 7:14, NASB).

The New Testament records the fulfillment of Isaiah's prophecy: "Now in the sixth month the angel Gabriel was sent from God to a city of Galilee, called Nazareth, to a virgin engaged to a man whose name was Joseph, of the descendants of David; and the virgin's name was Mary. . . . And the angel said to her, 'Do not be afraid, Mary; for you have found favor with God.

"And behold, you will conceive in your womb, and bear a son, and you shall name Him Jesus. . . .' And Mary said to the angel, 'How can this be, since I am a virgin?'

"And the angel answered and said to her, 'The Holy Spirit, will come upon you, and the power of the Most High will overshadow you; and for that reason the holy offspring shall be called the Son of God. . . . For nothing will be impossible with God'" (Luke 1:27, 30, 31, 34, 35, 37, NASB).

The virgin birth is set down in the Bible as a historical fact. The writers who recorded the story were Matthew—an eyewitness to the events in the life of Jesus—and Luke, the doctor, who presents many things in the life of Christ from the viewpoint of His mother, Mary.

The passages in both Matthew and Luke are authentic, with no evidence at all that they were later additions to the text. The doctrine of the virgin birth has been believed by the church from its beginning.

Ignatius, who lived at the beginning of the second century, wrote to the Ephesians and said, "For our God, Jesus the Christ, was conceived in the womb by Mary, according to a dispensation, of the seed of David but also of the Holy Ghost."

There are several reasons why the virgin birth was a necessity. The Bible teaches that the Word who became flesh was with God from the very beginning (John 1:1). The fact of the pre-existence of Christ is testified many times in the New Testament (John 8:58; Philippians 2:5–11; Colossians 1:15, 16).

When Jesus came into the world, He was not a newly created individual such as we are, but was rather the eternal Son of God. To be born into this world of the virgin Mary required divine intervention, and this is exactly what the Gospels record.

Another reason why Jesus needed to be virgin-born was because of His sinless nature. A basic New Testament teaching is that from the day He was born until the day He died, Jesus was without sin. To be a perfect sacrifice, He must Himself be perfect—without sin. Since our race is contaminated with sin, a miraculous entrance into the world would be required, hence the virgin birth.

Moreover, if Jesus had been sired by Joseph, He would not have been able to assume the throne of David. According to the prophecy of Jeremiah 22:28–30, there could be no king in Israel who was a descendant of King Jeconiah, and Matthew 1:12 relates that Joseph was from the line of Jeconiah. If Jesus had been fathered by Joseph, He could not rightly inherit the throne of David, since he was a relative of the cursed line.

The virgin birth of Christ is not only a historical fact, but it was also a *necessary* historical fact when one considers all the data.

Aren't there legitimate objections to the virgin birth which make it un- believable to us today?

There are possibly other ways which God could have chosen to send His Son into the world, but the fact is the way He chose to do it was through the virgin birth.

The Gospels record that Mary and Joseph did not have sexual relations until after Christ was born, and he "kept her a virgin until she gave birth to a Son; and he called His name Jesus" (Matthew 1:25, NASB).

The New Testament also relates that Joseph was known not to have fathered Jesus and that most people had assumed Mary had an illicit relationship with someone.

Even though the virgin birth is given as a historical fact and certain things made the virgin birth essential, many still voice loud objections to its occurrence.

The main problem that people have with the virgin birth is that it is a miracle. Scripture does not treat this event as an ordinary occurrence but rather as a supernatural act of God. The miracle of the virgin birth should not pose any special problem if one grants the possibility of miracles.

Why, we may ask, is the virgin birth any greater miracle than say the feeding of the 5,000 or Jesus walking on water? If an all-powerful God does exist, who spoke all creation into existence, a virgin birth would not be beyond His capability.

A common objection to the virgin birth is that it is a biological impossibility, which was accepted by people ignorant of these things. C. S. Lewis made some pertinent observations in this view:

"Thus you will hear people say, 'The early Christians believed that Christ was the son of a virgin, but we know that this is a scientific impossibility.' Such people seem to have an idea that belief in miracles arose at a period when men were so ignorant of the course of nature that they did not perceive a miracle to be contrary to it.

"A moment's thought shows this to be foolish, with the story of the virgin birth as a particularly striking example. When Joseph discovered that his fiancée was going to have a baby, he not unnaturally decided to repudiate her. Why? Because he knew just as well as any modern gynecologist that in the ordinary course of nature women do not have babies unless they have lain with men.

"No doubt the modern gynecologist knows several things about birth and begetting which Joseph did not know. But those things do not concern the main point—that a virgin birth is contrary to the course of nature. And Joseph obviously knew that" (*Miracles*, New York, Macmillan Pub. Co. Inc., p. 48).

Some have attempted to account for the virgin birth by tracing it to Greek or Babylonian mythology. They argue that the Gospel writers borrowed this story from the mythology of their day. This view does not fit the facts, for there is not any hero in pagan mythology for which a virgin birth is claimed, and moreover it would be unthinkable to the Jewish mind to construct such a story from mythology.

Many deities among the Greeks, Babylonians, and Egyptians were reported born in an unusual manner, but for the most part these beings never actually existed. The accounts are filled with obvious mythological elements which are totally absent from the Gospel narratives. They are reports of a god or goddess being born into the world by sexual relations between some heavenly being and an earthly woman, or by some adulterous affair among the gods and goddesses.

Dr. Thomas Thorburn comments appropriately, "All these various stories of supernatural conceptions and births, which we meet with in folklore and the history of mythology, have this one point in common—they serve to point not so much to the similarity as to the complete contrast and dissimilarity which exists between the Christian birth-story and the tales which are current in various pagan circles" (Thomas James

Thorburn, *A Critical Examination of the Evidences for the Doctrine of the Virgin Birth*, London, 1908, p. 158).

Thus when we closely consider the objections to the virgin birth, we become more convinced that it did indeed occur just as the historical record in the Gospel states.

✚ ADDITIONAL REFERENCE SOURCES

Wilbur Smith, *The Supernaturalness of Christ*, W.A. Wilde Co., 1954

J. Gresham Machen, *The Virgin Birth of Christ*, New York, Harper and Brothers, 19930

Robert Gromacki, *The Virgin Birth*, New York, Thomas Nelson, Inc., 1974

Arthur Custance, *The Virgin Birth and the Incarnation*, Grand Rapids, Zondervan, 1976

Aren't the genealogies of Jesus given in Matthew and Luke contradictory?

A question that has longed perplexed the readers of the New Testament concerns the differing genealogies of Jesus Christ recorded in Matthew 1 and Luke 3.

At first glance, the impression is created that both accounts are tracing the family line of Jesus through His earthly father Joseph in which case we would be faced with an obvious contradiction, because Matthew 1:16 indicates Jacob is Joseph's father, while Luke 3:23 tells us that Heli is the father of Joseph.

A plausible solution to this difficulty is to understand that Matthew is indeed giving us Joseph's family line, but Luke is tracing the genealogy of Mary. The reason that Mary is not mentioned in Luke 3 is because she has already been designated the mother of Jesus in several instances.

The usual practice of a Jewish genealogy is to give the name of the father, grandfather, etc., of the person in view. Luke follows this pattern, and does not mention the name of Mary, but the name of the legal father. However, Luke is quick to add that Joseph is not, in reality, the father of Jesus, since Jesus had been virgin born (Luke 1:34, 35).

A literal translation of Luke 3:23 would be, "Jesus, when He began, was about thirty years old, being the son of Joseph, as it was thought, of Heli. . . ." This does not at all mean that Jesus was the son of Heli, but that Jesus was a descendant, on His mother's side, of Heli. The word "son" has this wider meaning.

Thus Luke is tracing the roots of Jesus through His mother, Mary, who was a descendant of Heli, etc. Joseph's name is mentioned, according to the common practice, but he is clearly portrayed as the *supposed* father of Jesus, and God as the actual father.

The purpose of the two genealogies is to demonstrate that Jesus was in the complete sense a descendant of David. Through His foster father, Joseph, He inherited—by law—the royal line, albeit a deposed line according to Jeremiah 22:28–30. More importantly through His mother He was a flesh and blood descendant of King David through David's son Nathan. Thus, Jesus had the proper credentials for the throne of David.

✚ ADDITIONAL REFERENCE SOURCES

Clark Pinnock, "Genealogy of Jesus Christ" in *Zondervan Pictorial Encyclopedia of the Bible*, Zondervan, Grand Rapids, 1975.

W. F. Arndt, *Does the Bible Contradict Itself?* 5th rev. ed., Concordia Press, 1955

Why is Jesus the only way to get to God?

 People are constantly asking, "What's so special about Jesus? Why is He the only way that someone can know God?"

Along with the problem of the heathen, there is no question asked more often than this one. We are accused of being narrow-minded because we assert there is no other way to get to God.

The first point to make is that we did not invent the claim of Jesus being the only way. This is not our claim; it is His. We are merely relating His claim, and the claim of the writers of the New Testament.

Jesus said, "I am the way, and the truth, and the life; no one comes to the Father, but through Me" (John 14:6, NASB) and, "For unless you believe that I am He, you shall die in your sins" (John 8:24, NASB). The apostle Peter echoed these words, "Neither is there salvation in any other: for there is none other name under heaven given among men, whereby we must be saved" (Acts 4:12, KJV).

St. Paul concurred, "There is one God, and one mediator between God and men, the man Christ Jesus . . . ." (I Timothy 2:5, KJV). It is therefore the united testimony of the New Testament that no one can know God the Father except through the person of Jesus Christ.

To understand why this is so, we must go back to the beginning. An infinite-personal God created the heavens and the earth (Genesis 1:1) and man in his own image (Genesis 1:26). When He had finished creating, everything was good (Genesis 1:31).

Man and woman were placed in a perfect environment, with all their needs taken care of. They were given only one prohibition; they were not to eat of the fruit of the tree of the knowledge of good and evil, lest they die (Genesis 2:17). Unfortunately, they did eat of the tree (Genesis 3), and the result was a fall in four different areas. The relationship between God and man was now broken, as can be seen from Adam's and Eve's attempting to hide from God (Genesis 3:8).

The relationship between man and his fellow man was severed, with both Adam and Eve arguing and trying to pass the blame to someone else (Genesis 3:12, 13).

The bond between man and nature also was broken, with the ground producing thorns and thistles and the animal world no longer being benevolent (Genesis 3:17, 18). Man also became separated from himself, with a feeling of emptiness and incompleteness, something he had not experienced before the fall.

However, God promised to make all these things right and gave His word that He would send a Saviour, or Messiah, who would deliver the entire creation from the bondage of sin (Genesis 3:15). The Old Testament kept repeating the theme that some day this person would come into the world and set mankind free.

God's Word did indeed come true. God became a man in the person of Jesus Christ (John 1:14, 29). Jesus eventually died in our place in order that we could enjoy again a right relationship with God. The Bible says, "God was in Christ, reconciling the world unto himself" and "he hath made him to be sin for us, who knew no sin; that we might be made the righteousness of God in him" (II Corinthians 5:19, 21, KJV).

Jesus has paved the way! God has done it all, and our responsibility is to accept that fact. We can do nothing to add to the work of Jesus; it has all been done for us.

If mankind could have reached God any other way, then Jesus would not have had to die. His death illustrates the fact that there is no other way. Therefore, no other religion or religious leader can bring someone to the knowledge of the one true God.

But the death of Jesus is not the end of the story. Let us illustrate why we prefer Jesus over other religious leaders. Suppose a group of us are taking a hike in a very dense forest. As we get deeper into the forest, we become lost.

Realizing that taking the wrong path now might mean we will lose our lives, we begin to be afraid. However, we soon notice that ahead in the distance where the trail splits, there are two human forms at the fork in the road.

Running up to these people, we notice that one has on a park ranger uniform, and he is standing there perfectly healthy and alive, while the other person is lying face down, dead. Now which of these two are we going to ask about the way out? Obviously, the one who is living.

When it comes to eternal matters, we are going to ask the one who is alive the way out of the predicament. This is not Mohammed, not Confucius, but Jesus Christ. Jesus is unique. He came back from the dead. This demonstrates He is the one whom He claimed to be (Romans 1:4), the unique Son of God and the only way by which a person can have a personal relationship with the true and living God.

✚ ADDITIONAL REFERENCE SOURCES

Don Stewart, "What's so Special About Jesus" (tape), The Word for Today, P.O. Box 8000, Costa Mesa, Calif. 92626

Josh McDowell, *More Than a Carpenter*, Tyndale House, 1977

How do you know that God exists?

Is there truly a God? How can anyone be sure such a being exists?

We believe that the existence of God, and questions such as these relating to it, can be intelligently answered. The reason we know that God exists is because He has told us so, and has revealed Himself to us.

It would be no help to us at all in our human predicament if God were silent, but happily this is not the case. God not only exists, but also He has communicated that fact to us. He has told us all about who He is, what He is like, and what His plan is for planet earth.

He has revealed these things to mankind through the Bible. The Bible has demonstrated itself to be more than a mere book; it is the actual Word of God. The evidence is more than convincing to anyone who will honestly consider its claims.

Because of the boasts the Bible makes for itself, many have tried to destroy it, as related in this statement by Martin Luther:

"Mighty potentates have raged against this book, and sought to destroy and uproot it—Alexander the Great and princes of Egypt and Babylon, the monarchs of Persia, of Greece and of Rome, the Emperors Julius and Augustus—but they prevailed nothing.

"They are gone while the book remains, and it will remain forever and ever, perfect and entire, as it was declared at first. Who has thus helped it—who has protected it against such mighty forces? No one, surely, but God Himself, who is master of all things" (Cited by Fritz Ridenour, *Who says*, G. L. Publications, Regal Books, 1967).

Even the French skeptic, Rousseau, saw something different in the Scriptures. "I must confess to you that the majesty of the Scriptures astonishes me; the holiness of the evangelists speaks to my heart and has such striking characters of truth, and is, moreover, so perfectly inimitable, that if it had been the invention of men, the inventors would be greater than the greatest heroes" (*Encyclopedia of Religious Quotations*, Frank Mead, p. 32).

The Bible, therefore, gives us sufficient reason to believe that it is the Word of the living God, who does exist and who has revealed Himself to the world.

Another reason that we know God exists is because He has appeared in human flesh. Jesus Christ was God Almighty who became a man. The Bible says, "The Word became flesh and dwelt among us" (John 1:14, RSV), and it is clear about the fact that Jesus came to earth to reveal who God is and what He is all about (John 1:18).

If someone wants to know who God is and what He is like, he only needs to look at Jesus Christ. As Lord Byron said, "If ever man was God or God was man, Jesus Christ was both" (*Encyclopedia of Religious Quotations*, Frank Mead, p. 81).

Instead of man reaching up to find God, God reached down to man, as Casserley explains, "The gospel provides that knowledge of ultimate truth which men have sought through philosophy in vain, inevitably in vain, because it is essential to the very nature of God that He cannot be discovered by searching and probing of human minds, that He can only be known if He first takes the initiative and reveals Himself" (J. V. Langmead Casserley, *The Christian in Philosophy*, New York, Charles Scribner's Sons, 1951, p. 21).

Jesus, in coming back from the dead, established Himself as having the credentials to be God, and it was this fact that demonstrated its truth to the unbelieving world. As Machen says, "The great weapon with which the disciples of Jesus set out to conquer the world was not a mere comprehension of eternal principles; it was a historical message, an account of something that had happened; it was the message, 'He is risen'" (J. G. Machen, *Christianity and Liberalism*, pp. 28, 29).

Thus we have the Bible, and the person of Jesus Christ, as two strong reasons arguing for the existence of God. No other religion or philosophy offers anything near to demonstrate that a God exists.

✚ ADDITIONAL REFERENCE SOURCES

Francis Schaeffer, *He Is There and He Is Not Silent*, Tyndale, House, 1972

Francis Schaeffer, *The God Who Is There*, Inter-Varsity, 1974

Norman Geisler, *Philosophy of Religion*, Zondervan, 1974

William Lane Craig, *The Existence of God and the Beginning of the Universe*, Here's Life Publishers, 1979

James Sire, *The Universe Next Door*, Inter-Varsity Press, 1976

Alvin Plantinga, *God and Other Minds*, Ithaca, New York, Cornell Univ. Press, 1967

Q Where did God come from? What was He doing before He created the universe?

 These questions assume that everything, including God, is subject to the limitations of time and space, as man is; that there is nothing outside of time and space, an assumption that the scientific community has questioned and virtually dismissed since Albert Einstein's theory of relativity.

Einstein showed that time can actually be altered, slowed down, speeded up, when objects begin to travel at extremely high speeds. This would suggest that the common concept that all things originate and operate within the context of fixed time and space, that nothing exists outside of time and space, is not necessarily correct.

While not totally understandable, the facts do make it easier to accept the biblical teaching that God exists outside of time and space as we know it (Psalms 90:4; Colossians 1:17; II Peter 3:8). To accept that God exists outside the time and space framework as we know it renders any question of where He came from and what He was doing before He created what we know as the universe totally meaningless.

These questions might be legitimate if God is subject to time and space, which He is not. The Bible teaches that God is not bound by time or space, and that He has not chosen to reveal to us (from our perspective) all that took place before He created the universe.

✚ ADDITIONAL REFERENCE SOURCES

John Warwick Montgomery, *How Do We Know There Is a God?* Bethany Fellowship, 1972

Francis Schaeffer, *Genesis in Space and Time*, Inter-Varsity Press, 1972

Isn't the God of the Old Testament a God of hate while the God of the New Testament is one of love?

Another of the frequent accusations against the Bible is that it contains two different conceptions of God. The Old Testament allegedly presents only a God of wrath, while the New Testament allegedly depicts only a God of love.

The Old Testament contains stories of God's commanding the destruction of Sodom, the annihilation of the Canaanites, and many other stories of God's judgment and wrath. The accusers claim this demonstrates a primitive, warlike deity in contradistinction to the advanced teachings of Jesus to love one another and to turn the other cheek, as contained in the Sermon on the Mount.

These ideas about God seem to be in direct conflict, but a moment's reflection will show otherwise. Jesus Himself declared that the Old Testament may be summed up by the commandments to love God and love your neighbor (Matthew 22:37). He also observed that God in the Old Testament had continually desired love and mercy rather than sacrifice (Matthew 9:13; 12:7).

This attitude can be seen with statements such as, "Have I any pleasure in the death of the wicked . . . and not rather that he should turn from his way and live?" (Ezekiel 18:23, RSV).

God would not have destroyed certain nations except that He is a God of justice and their evil could not go unchecked and condoned.

He did intend and desire to punish them as a part of His plan, in consistency with His holy nature and jealousy for His wayfaring people. What He desires in consistency with His pure character, He does in justice, in their case, providing they have not repented and come into harmony with His nature (Jeremiah 18).

In the case of the Amorites, God gave them hundreds of years to repent, yet they did not (Genesis 15:16). Noah preached 120 years to his generation before the great flood (Genesis 6:3). The proper Old Testament picture is one of a very patient God who gives these people untold opportunities to repent and come into harmony with Him, and only when they continually refuse does He judge and punish them for their evil deeds.

Contrary to some popular belief, the strongest statements of judgment and wrath in the Bible were made by the Lord Jesus Himself. In Matthew 23, for example, He lashed out at the religious leaders of His day, calling them hypocrites and false leaders, and informing them that their destiny was eternal banishment from God's presence.

In Matthew 10:34 (KJV), Jesus says that the purpose of His mission is not to unite but to divide. "Think not that I am come to send peace on earth: I came not to send peace, but a sword." He goes on to say that His word will cause a father to be against his son, a mother against her daughter, and a daughter-in-law against her mother-in-law (Matthew 10:35).

We find judgment as well as love scattered very pervasively throughout the New Testament, and love and mercy as well as judgment throughout the Old Testament. God is consistent and unchanging, but different situations call for different emphases. Therefore, when the two testaments are read the way they were intended, they reveal the same holy God who is rich in mercy, but who will not let sin go unpunished.

What is the Trinity? Do Christians worship three Gods?

One of the most misunderstood ideas in the Bible concerns the teaching about the Trinity. Although Christians say that they believe in one God, they are constantly accused of polytheism (worshiping at least three gods).

The Scriptures do *not* teach that there are three Gods; neither do they teach that God wears three different masks while acting out the drama of history. What the Bible does teach is stated in the doctrine of the Trinity as: there is *one* God who has revealed Himself in three persons, the Father, the Son, and the Holy Spirit, and these three persons are the one God.

Although this is difficult to comprehend, it is nevertheless what the Bible tells us, and is the closest the finite mind can come to explaining the infinite mystery of the infinite God, when considering the biblical statements about God's being.

The Bible teaches that there is one God and only one God: "Hear, O Israel! The Lord is our God, the Lord is one!" (Deuteronomy 6:4, NASB). "There is one God" (I Timothy 2:5, KJV). "Thus says the Lord, the King of Israel and his Redeemer, the Lord of hosts: I am the first and I am the last, and there is no God besides Me'" (Isaiah 44:6, NASB).

However, even though God is one in His essential being or nature, He is also three persons. "Let us make man in our image" (Genesis 1:26, KJV). "God said, 'Behold, the man has become like one of us'" (Genesis 3:22, RSV).

God's plural nature is alluded to here, for He could not be talking to angels in these instances, because angels could not and did not help God create. The Bible teaches that Jesus

Christ, not the angels, created all things (I John 1:3; Colossians 1:15; Hebrews 1:2).

In addition to speaking of God as one, and alluding to a plurality of God's being, the Scriptures are quite specific as to naming God in terms of three persons. There is a person whom the Bible calls the Father, and the Father is designated as God the Father (Galatians 1:1).

The Bible talks about a person named Jesus, or the Son, or the Word, also called God. "The Word was God . . ." (John 1:1, KJV). Jesus was "also calling God His own Father, making Himself equal with God" (John 5:18, NASB).

There is a third person mentioned in the Scriptures called the Holy Spirit, and this person—different from the Father and the Son—is also called God ("Ananias, why has Satan filled your heart to lie to the Holy Spirit? . . . You have not lied to men but to God" (Acts 5:3, 4, RSV).

The facts of the biblical teaching are these: There is one God. This one God has a plural nature. This one God is called the Father, the Son, the Holy Spirit, all distinct personalities, all designated God. We are therefore led to the conclusion that the Father, Son, and Holy Spirit are one God, the doctrine of the Trinity.

Dr. John Warwick Montgomery offers this analogy to help us understand this doctrine better:

"The doctrine of the Trinity is not 'irrational'; what *is* irrational is to suppress the biblical evidence for Trinity in favor of unity, or the evidence for unity in favor of Trinity.

"Our data must take precedence over our models—or, stating it better, our models must sensitively reflect the full range of data.

"A close analogy to the theologian's procedure here lies in the work of the theoretical physicist: Subatomic entities are found, on examination, to possess wave properties (W), particle properties (P), and quantum properties (h).

"Though these characteristics are in many respects incompatible (particles don't diffract, while waves do, etc.), physicists 'explain' or 'model' an electron as PWh. They have to do this in order to give proper weight to all the relevant data.

"Likewise the theologian who speaks of God as 'three in one.' Neither the scientist nor the theologian expects you to get a 'picture' by way of his model; the purpose of the model is to help you take into account *all* of the facts, instead of perverting reality through super-imposing an apparent 'consistency' on it.

"The choice is clear: either the Trinity or a 'God' who is only a pale imitation of the Lord of biblical and confessional Christianity" (*How Do We Know There Is a God*, pp. 14, 15).

✚ ADDITIONAL REFERENCE SOURCES

John Warwick Montgomery, *How Do We Know There Is a God?* Bethany Fellowship, 1972

Kenneth Boa, *God, I Don't Understand*, Victor Books, 1975

Walter Martin, "Jehovah's Witnesses, Jesus Christ and the Holy Trinity" (tape) Christian Research, Box 500, San Juan Capistrano, Calif. 92693

Q

Why are the biblical miracles different from those in other accounts of the miraculous?

Some people feel that the miracles recorded in the Bible betray the fact that the Scriptures are to be taken seriously. They are compared to Greek mythology and other tales of both the supernatural and bizarre. Instead of investigating their foundation, they class them immediately with legends and folklore.

Admittedly, there are many stories from our Lord's day among the Greeks and Romans which are so fanciful and ridiculous that they are not worthy of serious consideration. This is in complete contrast to the biblical miracles, which never offer a mindless display of the supernatural.

To simply say that, because *some* reported supernatural events are ridiculous and untrue, therefore *any* reported supernatural occurrence or miracle is untrue denotes faulty reasoning. It is "guilt" by association, or a case of throwing the baby out with the bath water.

Of the words used in the New Testament for miracles, the common words are those expressing the ideas of "supernatural powers." These are the words used not only by the New Testament authors, but also by the Greek and Roman writers in their stories and myths. However, in the biblical account an additional word is used, wich is seldom if at all used by the Greek and Roman authors.

The word used is "sign," which means attesting miracle or a miraculous proof. John states at the end of his Gospel, "Many other signs therefore Jesus also performed in the presence of the disciples, which are not written in this book; but these have been written that you may believe that Jesus is the Christ, the

Son of God; and that believing you may have life in His name" (John 20:30, 31, NASB).

The miracle stories as recorded in the Bible are always for a definite purpose and never to show off. There is always a logical reason for them. For example, there were 5,000 people who were in immediate need of food, which was promptly provided by miraculous means (Luke 9:12–17).

At a wedding feast in Cana, the wine had run out. The need for wine was met by Jesus, who turned water into wine (John 2:1–11). The miracles of Jesus were performed out of love and compassion to those who were afflicted. They were also meant to be objective signs to the people that He was the promised Messiah, since one of the credentials of the Messiah would be signs and miracles.

Jesus pointed out this fact when questioned by two messengers of John the Baptist about his identity. "Go and shew John again those things which ye do hear and see: The blind receive their sight, and the lame walk, the lepers are cleansed, and the deaf hear, the dead are raised up, and the poor have the gospel preached to them" (Matthew 11:4, 5, KJV).

When reading the miraculous accounts in the Bible and especially in the Gospels, a person has to note the fact that the miracles weren't denied by the critics. In the life and ministry of Jesus, He was never asked if He performed miracles; He was always asked how He was able to do them. They wanted to know where He derived the power and authority (Matthew 21:23).

It was impossible for them to deny that He was doing miraculous things; literally hundreds of people had been cured, and there was no other explanation. The fact of His miracles was not in dispute. They couldn't be denied.

On the day of Pentecost, less than two months after the crucifixion of Jesus, Simon Peter told a large gathering, "Jesus of Nazareth, a man approved of God among you by miracles and wonders and signs, which God did by him in the midst of you, as ye yourselves also know" (Acts 2:22, KJV).

Peter here, in front of a hostile crowd, states that the people themselves were aware of the miracles of Jesus. Just the fact that he wasn't immediately shouted down demonstrates that the wonders Jesus performed were well known to everyone.

The first hand testimony to the miraculous is something that does not occur either in other religions or in Greek or Roman mythology. The straightforward account of the supernatural works breaking into the natural order are recorded for us in the Bible by eyewitnesses to these events.

All of these considerations demonstrate the qualitative difference of the biblical miracles. It is important now to consider why miracles are rejected. One reason why these miracles are rejected is because they do not fit with many people's view of the world. They have never witnessed a miracle, and they conclude therefore that miracles cannot happen or that they are impossible.

Instead of investigating the evidence for the miraculous, the whole idea is ruled out ahead of time as being totally impossible. This is not a proper way to deal with this issue, since only a person with all knowledge of events past, present, and future could exclude the possibility of miracles.

There is an appropriate historical example of this folly of ruling out something ahead of time because it does not fit with one's view of the world. When explorers first came to Australia, they encountered an animal that defied all known laws of taxonomy. They discovered a semiaquatic, egg-laying mammal, having a broad, flat tail, webbed feet and a snout resembling a duck's bill. They named this animal the platypus.

Upon returning to their native land, they related their finding to the world. The people regarded their report as a hoax, since no such animal with the above characteristics could possibly exist. Even though there was reputable eyewitness testimony, it was rejected because of their world view.

They went back a second time to Australia, and returned with the hide of a dead platypus. The people accused them of rigging a hoax again. It seems that those people took Benjamin Disraeli's dictum seriously, "I make it a rule only to believe what I understand" (*The Infernal Marriage*, Pt. 1, Ch. 4). However, as Charles Caleb Colton has pointed out, "He that will believe only what he can fully comprehend must have a very long head or a very short creed" (Frank Mead, *Encyclopedia of Religious Quotations,* p. 17).

Many people, unfortunately, hold this type of attitude and determine the verdict before examining the evidence. This attitude is not only unscientific, but also it can be dangerous to the one holding the view. If there is a God, and if He has revealed Himself through the miraculous, then an individual is cutting off his only chance of finding this out.

By refusing to accept the possibility of God breaking into history in a supernatural way, he is destroying his only hope of understanding what life is all about. Therefore, it is of the highest importance at least to look into the possibility of miracles occurring because of the eternal stakes which are in view. There are indeed "more things in heaven and earth, Horatio, than are dreamt of in our philosophy."

✚ ADDITIONAL REFERENCE SOURCES

Wilbur Smith, *The Supernaturalness of Christ,* W.A. Wilde Company, 1954

C. S. Lewis, Miracles: *A Preliminary Study,* New York, Macmillan Publishing Company, 1960

John Warwick Montgomery, *Faith Founded on Fact,* Thomas Nelson & Sons, 1978

Gordon Clark, "Miracles," *Zondervan Pictorial Encyclopedia of the Bible,* vol. 4, Merrill Tenney, editor, Zondervan, Grand Rapids, 1975, pp. 241–250

Arlie J. Hoover, *Dear Agnos,* Grand Rapids, Baker Book House, 1976

Bernard Ramm, *Protestant Christian Evidences,* chapters 2, 4, 5, Moody Press, 1954

Q

Were the biblical miracles magic tricks which fooled the simple, primitive people?

A

It is often contended that people who lived during biblical times were more simple minded and superstitious than modern man, and could be tricked into believing the miraculous stories contained in the Bible.

Today it is claimed we live in a scientific age and have outgrown these superstitions, since we have developed the mental capacity to see these miracles as being superstitious myths rather than paranormal phenomena. A close study of the evidence will show that these accounts are not a superstitious reaction to some clever trickster. The response to the miraculous acts of God show the same surprise and anxiety that modern man would have if he were placed in the same situation.

The people living at the time of Jesus certainly knew that men born blind do not immediately receive their sight (John 9:32), that five loaves and a few fish would not feed 5,000 people (John 6:14), or that men do not walk on water (Matthew 14:26).

Doubting Thomas said, "Unless I see in his hands the print of the nails, and place my finger in the mark of the nails, and place my hand in his side, I will not believe" (John 20:25, RSV). He refused to accept the testimony of the unbelievable event of the resurrection, but changed his mind when confronted face-to-face with the resurrected Christ. Thus we are not expected to believe the ridiculous, and neither were the people of biblical times.

The people living in those times were no less skeptical than we are today. It was the unavoidable, the inescapable, the irrefutable fact that caused them to believe. The natural order was interfered with as a miracle occurred. It is only the skepticism of modern man that causes him to deny that miracles occurred.

How can miracles be possible?

The following statements, one ancient and one modern, are typical of the response people make to the miraculous.

"For nothing can happen without cause; nothing happens that cannot happen, and when what was capable of happening has happened, it may not be interpreted as a miracle. Consequently, there are no miracles. . . . We therefore draw this conclusion: what was capable of happening is not a miracle" (Cicero, *De Divinatione*, 2. 28, cited by V. van der Loos in *The Miracle of Jesus*, Leiden: E. J. Brill, 1965, p. 7).

"For example, there is the record of the life of Jesus Christ in the Bible. That record contained accounts of events which, in light of the facts of the natural order which were known, could not possibly have happened.

"Children are not born to virgins, angels do not bring messages to people, men do not walk on water, people who die do not return to life, and so on.

"The story of Jesus Christ was filled with what men had learned were impossibilities; therefore, the story could not be a literal account of the actual happenings.

"When the New Testament was written, men may have been naive enough to believe the things that were said about Jesus, and they may have seen no contradiction between the reports and their knowledge of the world, but now all was otherwise" (*Protestantism*, cited by J. Leslie Dunstan, Washington Square Press, Inc., New York, 1962, pp. 128–129).

Many laugh at the idea of the possibility of miracles. They argue that miracles are a violation of scientific laws and are therefore unacceptable to modern man.

The Scriptures, however, from one end to the other, contain stories of the miraculous. There are accounts of blind people who immediately received their sight, dead people being raised and extraordinary occurrences within nature, such as a universal flood and the parting of the Red Sea.

The basis for believing in the miraculous goes back to the biblical conception of God. The very first verse of the Bible decides the issue. "In the beginning God created the heavens and the earth" (Genesis 1:1, RSV).

If this verse can be accepted at face value, that in the beginning an infinite-personal God created the universe, then the rest should not be a problem. If He has the ability to do this, then a virgin birth, walking on water, feeding 5,000 people with a few loaves and fish, and the other biblical miracles become not only possible but expected.

Of course, if one does not believe in God, he will not accept the miraculous, but for those who have granted the *possibility* it is not at all ridiculous. As the apostle Paul once said to an unbelieving king, "Why should it be thought a thing incredible with you, that God should raise the dead?" (Acts 26:8, KJV).

So behind this important question is the familiar issue of whether or not God exists. For if there is a God, then certainly miracles are possible. In fact, the very nature of the question: "How can miracles be possible?" presupposes there is a God, for a miracle is an act of God.

As for the idea that miracles violate natural or scientific laws, we must remember that scientific laws neither dictate events nor do they explain them. They are merely a generalization about observable causes and effects.

One cannot reject the claim of the parting of the Red Sea 3,500 years ago by noting that this even does not happen every day. Appealing to the laws of nature to refute the miraculous will not work, since the Bible teaches that an all-powerful God has broken into the natural order from time to time with His mighty acts.

A miracle is by definition an event that is unique and without a precedent. It is impossible to account for it as we do other events. The proper way of determining if something happened is not whether we can explain it. The first question to be asked is not can it happen, but rather did it happen?

If an event can be determined as having happened, yet it defies explanation, we still have to admit to the fact that it happened, explanation or not. The evidence for biblical miracles is as powerful historically as other historical events (such as the fall of Rome and the conquests of Alexander the Great). Just because miracles are outside of our normal daily experience does not mean that they have not occurred and do not occur.

Thus when all the evidence is taken into account, there are excellent reasons for believing not only in the possibility of miracles but also in their actuality.

Q

Doesn't Mark disagree with the other three Gospels about Peter's denial of Jesus?

A A problem that has perplexed many careful students of the Bible concerns the accounts of the denial of Christ by Simon Peter. Jesus said to Peter, "Truly I say to you that this very night, before a cock crows, you shall deny Me three times" (Matthew 26:34, NASB).

Matthew records the fulfillment of this prediction, "And immediately the cock crew. And Peter remembered the word of Jesus, which said unto him, Before the cock crow, thou shalt deny me thrice. And he went out, and wept bitterly" (Matthew 26:74, 75, KJV).

The problem comes when we read Mark's version, "and Jesus saith unto him, Verily I say unto thee, That this day, even in this night, before the cock crow twice, thou shalt deny me thrice" (Mark 14:30, KJV). The fulfillment reads, concerning Peter, "He went out into the porch" (Mark 14:68, KJV), and later, in verse 72, "the second time the cock crew."

Peter called to mind the word that Jesus said to him, "Before the cock crow *twice*, thou shalt deny me thrice. And when he thought thereon, he wept." Was it before the cock crowed once or twice that Peter denied Jesus? Luke and John give the same basic account as Matthew, making Mark's statement seemingly at variance with the other three.

This problem is not as unresolvable as it may seem. It is quite reasonable that Jesus made both statements. He told Peter that he would deny Him before the crowing of the cock, and his denial would occur before it had crowed twice.

What we have, therefore, is Mark recording the story in more detail. This would seem natural since Mark wrote his

Gospel under the influence of Simon Peter, and it would be natural for him to further detail this story, seeing that he is one of the main characters.

Thus we have all four evangelists recording that Jesus predicted Peter's denial of Jesus, with Mark adding further details. A possible reconstruction would be the following: Jesus reveals to Peter that before the cock crows, Peter will deny Him three times.

Peter, as was his way, probably objected loudly to this idea that he would deny his Lord. Jesus then in turn repeats His earlier prediction, along with a further note that before the cock crows twice Peter will deny Him three times. (This harmony fits well with Mark's account in his Gospel.)

Furthermore, the clause, "Before a cock crows, you shall deny Me three times" (Matthew 26:34, NASB), is not contradicted by Mark relating that after Peter had denied Jesus the first time, the cock crowed. The cock crow was the sign that morning was soon to appear, and the phrase, "the time of the cock crow," is another term for dawn.

When Jesus is referring to the cock crowing twice, he is predicting a crowing of the cock in the middle of the night long before daybreak.

"Observation over a period of 12 years in Jerusalem has confirmed that the cock crows at three distinct times, first about a half hour after midnight, a second time about an hour later, and a third time an hour after the second" (William Lane, *The Gospel According to Mark*, p. 543).

When all the facts are considered, the problem of Peter's denial is not at all a blatant contradiction, but can be harmonized.

✚ ADDITIONAL REFERENCE SOURCES

W. F. Arndt, *Does the Bible Contradict Itself?* Concordia Press, 5th rev. ed., 1955

Cheney Johnston, *The Life of Christ in Stereo*, Portland, Western Baptist Press, 1969

Q

How would you explain the inaccuracy between Judas hanging himself in Matthew 27:5 and "falling headlong he burst open" in Acts 1:18?

A This question of the manner in which Judas died is one with which we are constantly confronted in our travels. Many people point to the apparent discrepancy in the two accounts as an obvious, irreconcilable error.

Some have gone so far as to say that the idea of an inerrant Bible is destroyed by these contradictory accounts. However, this is not the case at all.

Matthew relates that Judas hanged himself, while Peter tells us he fell and was crushed by the impact. The two statements are indeed different, but do they necessarily contradict each other?

Matthew does not say that Judas did not fall; neither does Peter say that Judas did not hang himself. This is not a matter of one person calling something black and the other person calling it white. Both accounts can be true and supplementary.

A possible reconstruction would be this: Judas hanged himself on a tree on the edge of a precipice that overlooked the valley of Hinnom. After he hung there for some time, the limb of the tree snapped or the rope gave way and Judas fell down the ledge, mangling his body in the process.

The fall could have been before *or* after death as either would fit this explanation. This possibility is entirely natural when the terrain of the valley of Hinnom is examined. From the bottom of the valley, you can see rocky terraces twenty-five to forty feet in height and almost perpendicular.

There are still trees that grow around the ledges and a rocky pavement at the bottom. Therefore, it is easy to conclude that Judas struck one of the jagged rocks on his way down, tearing his body open. It is important to remember that we are not told how long Judas remained hanging from the tree or how advanced was the decomposition of his body before his fall.

Louis Gaussen relates a story of a man who was determined to kill himself. This individual placed himself on the sill of a high window and pointed a pistol at his head. He then pulled the trigger and leaped from the window at the same time.

On the one hand, a person could say that this man took his life by shooting himself, while another could rightly contend he committed suicide by jumping from the tall building. In this case, both are true, as both are true in the case of Matthew's and Peter's accounts of the death of Judas. It is merely a situation of different perspectives of the same event.

✚ ADDITIONAL REFERENCE SOURCES

W. F. Arndt, *Does the Bible Contradict Itself?* 5th rev. ed., Concordia Press, 1955

Louis Gaussen, *Theopneustia*, Gospel Union Pub. Co., 1912

Q

Doesn't Matthew make a mistake when he attributes a prophecy to Jeremiah when it was actually given by Zechariah?

In the Gospel according to Matthew, Judas Iscariot, after betraying Jesus, feels remorse because of his evil deeds and throws the betrayal money into the sanctuary and commits suicide. Matthew goes on to relate how this money was taken by the priests and used to buy a potter's field.

Matthew concludes, "Then was fulfilled that which was spoken by Jeremy the prophet, saying, And they took the thirty pieces of silver, the price of him that was valued . . . and gave them for the potter's field, as the Lord appointed me" (Matthew 27:9, 10, KJV).

The problem is that verse 9 attributes the prophecy to Jeremiah, when it appears that it was Zechariah who gave this prediction. When Matthew 27:9 is examined closely in light of Zechariah 11:12, 13, it is clear that this prophecy is the one fulfilled. Why then does Matthew assign it to Jeremiah?

Various solutions have been offered to solve this dilemma. One idea is that this was an oral statement of Jeremiah, but this cannot be proven, so should be disregarded. The Church historian, Eusebius, claimed that the Jews deleted this passage from the Book of Jeremiah, but this hardly fits with the way the Scriptures were revered by the Jews.

The scribes' reverence was so great that even when they found an obvious error, they refused to alter the text. Instead, they made a notation in the margin.

Some people just conclude that Matthew made an error, while others try to connect this prophecy with some part of

Jeremiah. There are those who claim that there was an early copyist error, with the original text actually reading Zechariah. This is mere conjecture.

A possible solution is Jeremiah's priority in the Talmud (Baba Bathra 14b, J. B. Lightfoot, *Horae Hebraicae et Talmudicae, II,* p. 362). Jeremiah was placed first in the ancient rabbinic order of the prophetic books. Matthew was then quoting from the collection of the books of the prophets, and cited Jeremiah since it was the first and therefore the identifier. The same thing is done in Luke 24:44, where Psalms is used when the entire third division of the Hebrew canon is in mind.

A problem with this solution is that the New Testament nowhere else cites a passage under the general name "Jeremiah." When Matthew elsewhere refers to Jeremiah, he gives a passage in Jeremiah itself (2:17), and when he mentions Isaiah he goes to passages in Isaiah (4:14; 8:17; 12:17, etc.).

Perhaps the best solution would be to understand that Matthew is combining two prophecies, one from Jeremiah and one from Zechariah, with a mention of only one author in the composite reference, namely Jeremiah, the major prophet.

Zechariah says nothing concerning the buying of a field, but Jeremiah states that the Lord appointed him to buy a field (Jeremiah 32:6–8) as a solemn guarantee by the Lord Himself that fields and vineyards would be bought and sold in the land in a future day (Jeremiah 32:15, 43ff).

One of the fields which God had in mind was the potter's field. Zechariah adds the details of the thirty pieces of silver and the money thrown down on the floor of the temple. Thus it can be seen that Matthew takes the detail of both prophets, but stresses Jeremiah as the one who foretold these occurrences.

Dr. J. E. Rosscup of Talbot Seminary adheres to a view consistent with the above. He points out:

"Matthew felt that two passages were fulfilled, one typical (Jeremiah 19:1–13) and one explicit (Zechariah 11:13), and mentions only one author in the composite reference, a practice that sometimes occurred, according to Robert Gundry

(*The Use of the Old Testament in St. Matthew's Gospel*, pp. 124–25).

"John N. Cool also concludes that Matthew used Zechariah chiefly, but had Jeremiah 19 prominently in mind as well, especially due to its theme of judgment on Israel ("A Study of Matthew 27:9, 10" M.A. thesis, Talbot, 1975, pp. 56–62, 66, 67).

"Cool says, 'Both (valley, Jeremiah 19; field, Matthew 27) became burial grounds and both their names are changed to remind the people of God's judgment. This . . . is . . . confirmed by the traditional location of the potter's field . . . within the valley of Hinnom where Jeremiah pronounced his judgment by changing its name to 'valley of slaughter.'

'Second, Matthew's consistent use of Isaiah and Jeremiah in his formula quotations reminds his readers of God's salvation and judgment for His people. Isaiah was associated with salvation, Jeremiah . . . with judgment.

'The use of *tote* in Matthew 2:17 and 27:9 instead of the purposeful *Hina* or *Houts* found in the other formula introductions also underscores the judgment motif by referring to Christ's enemies as fulfilling prophecy' (pp. 66, 67).

"Gundry says that Matthew's reference to Jeremiah in the introduction formula makes certain that readers will take note of the connection with Jeremiah 19, which might be overlooked" (p. 125).

✚ ADDITIONAL REFERENCE SOURCES

Charles Lee Feinberg, *God Remembers: A Study of Zechariah*, 3rd. ed., Portland, Oregon, Multnomah Press, 1977, pp. 214–217

Hobart Freeman, *An Introduction to the Old Testament Prophets*, Moody Press, 1969

How could all the animals fit in the Ark?

One of the objections to the biblical account of the flood concerns Noah getting all the animals into the ark. An examination of the dimensions of the ark, as given by the Bible, sheds considerable light on this account.

John Whitcomb and Henry Morris, in their book, *The Genesis Flood*, did an exceptionally thorough job of analyzing the pertinent data relating to the physical dimensions and carrying capacity of the ark. They note that the ark would have been 437.5 feet in length, 72.92 feet in width, and 43.75 feet in height (figuring from 17.5 inches per cubit).

The ark had three decks (Genesis 6:16), so the total deck area was approximately 95,700 square feet, and the total volume 1,396,000 cubic feet. The gross tonnage of the ark would be approximately 13,960 tons, which is comparable to some large, modern-day vessels.

The carrying capacity of the ark would, therefore, be equal to 522 standard railroad stock cars, each of which could carry 240 sheep. The ark could have accommodated at least 125,000 sheep. Additionally, Genesis 6:14 tells us that besides having three decks, nests or rooms were constructed to house the animals.

Whitcomb and Morris additionally determined, by examining "the best estimates of modern taxonomy," that there were less than 17,600 of the currently known species of mammals, birds, reptiles, and amphibians that would have needed the shelter of the ark.

Calculating for two of each on the ark, there would need to be room for only 35,200 animals, plus five each of clean animals (a very small number, but for the sake of argument, allow for half the species or 8,800 x 5 being 44,000), a total of 79,000 animals maximum would have been on the ark.

Since there were probably a small number of species (or kinds) originally (given the facts of animal husbandry, accounting for a great deal of the diversity in the animal kingdom today, and given the fact that most dry land animals are smaller than sheep, and that it can be assumed that young and therefore smaller animals were taken) it is not at all inconceivable for the ark to have held sufficient number of animals, with room for food stores.

The concept of having animals on the ark that had within themselves the gene pools that would allow for the development of many different kinds of animals we have today must not be overlooked. The animals on the ark could well have been literal "genetic banks" that through the years of proliferation developed the varieties of animals we see today, as Henry M. Morris states in his book *The Genesis Flood:*

" . . . a hundred years of . . . study in the science of zoology has brought to light some interesting facts concerning the amazing potentialities for diversification which the Creator has placed within the Genesis kinds. These 'kinds' have never evolved or merged into each other by crossing over the divinely-established lines of demarcation; but they have been diversified into so many varieties and sub-varieties (like the races and families of humanity) that even the greatest taxonomists have been staggered at the task of enumerating and classifying them.

"Frank Lewis Marsh . . . illustrates his conception of how some of the typical baramins (from *bara*—"created," and *min*—"kind") might have become diversified before and after the Flood. He points out that over 500 varieties of the sweet pea have been developed from a single type since the year 1700; and that over 200 distinct varieties of dogs, as different from each other as the dachshund and the collie, have developed from a very few wild dogs. In further discussing the matter, Dr. Marsh writes:

'In the field of zoology a very good illustration of descent with variation is furnished by the domestic pigeon. The diversity in form and temperament to be found among strains of pigeons would stagger our belief in their common origin if we did not know that they have all been developed from the wild rock pigeon of European coasts, *Columbia livia*. It is extremely interesting to see the variations from the ancestral form which are exhibited in such strains as the pouter, the leghorn runt, the fantail, the tumbler, the owl, the turbit, the swallow, the carrier, the nun, the jacobin, and the homer. Different "species" names and possibly even different "generic" names would certainly be assigned to some of these if it were not known that they are merely strains of a common stock.'"

✚ ADDITIONAL REFERENCE SOURCES

John Whitcomb and Henry Morris, *The Genesis Flood*, Presbyterian Reformed, 1961

How many of each animal entered the Ark?

A "And of every living thing of all flesh, you shall bring two of every kind into the ark, to keep them alive with you; they shall be male and female" (Genesis 6:19, 20, NASB).

"You shall take with you of every clean animal by sevens, a male and his female; and of the animals that are not clean two, a male and his female; also of the birds of the sky, by sevens, male and female, to keep offspring alive on the face of all the earth" (Genesis 7:2, 3, NASB).

"Of clean animals and animals that are not clean and birds and everything that creeps on the ground, there went into the ark to Noah by twos, male and female, as God had commanded Noah" (Genesis 7:8, 9, NASB).

At first reading, the statements appear to be contradictory. First (Genesis 6:19, 20) Noah is commanded to bring two of every kind into the ark, then in Genesis 7:2, 3, seven of some animals and birds, and then later in 7:8, 9, the Scriptures speak of animals going in by twos.

However, Genesis 7:8, 9 does not speak of the *numbers* of animals going in, but the *manner*. Seven of each clean animal (three pairs, with another animal to be used for sacrifice) marched into the ark by twos, and the other animals also went in by pairs.

The remaining question of the possible contradiction between Genesis 6:19, 20 and Genesis 7:2, 3 is easily resolved when they are understood in light of the literary practices of the ancients. A general statement would be made first, and then followed with another statement providing specifics.

This is the case here, with Genesis 6:19, 20 being the general statement and Genesis 7:2, 3 providing the additional detail that clean animals were to be taken by sevens, instead of just by twos as were the other animals. A male and a female, two of each kind, entered with an additional five of each clean animal.

✝   ADDITIONAL REFERENCE SOURCES

H.C. Leupold, *Exposition of Genesis*, Vol. I, Baker Book House, 1958

John J. Davis, *Paradise to Prison*, Baker Book House, 1975

Henry M. Morris, *The Genesis Record*, Baker Book House, 1976

Q Where do dinosaurs and other extinct animals fit into the biblical story?

A Very few of the many species of animals are mentioned in the Bible. Genesis records only that God created all living creatures of the sea, of the earth, and of the sky, and labels them in the most general terms: cattle and creeping things and beasts of the earth and winged creatures.

Only those animals that are significant to human history are mentioned in the Bible specifically, such as cattle, oxen, goats, sheep (important to the economy), plus the specific list of clean and unclean animals in the Levitical law, etc. Many animals are not specifically named in the Bible, dinosaurs among them.

Lack of mention means little, other than that they did not come into the history of man in a way significant or necessary to record. That dinosaurs existed is apparent from the fossil records of the great dinosaur beds, presumably preserved by a catastrophe, such as the flood.

Unless the sediments which entrapped them hardened quickly into stone, their bodies would have soon decomposed, but the remains that we have are whole bodies intact. A catastrophe such as the flood would explain having such remains.

Additional evidence for their existence, and at the same time as man, is the pictographs left in Africa and North America, and from fossil evidence of human and dinosaur footprints in the same formation.

As to why and how they became extinct, we can only conjecture. We do know that Genesis records that when God finished creation, everything was very good. When the fall occurred, death and destruction entered the universe.

Eventually, corruption was so widespread that God destroyed all but Noah's family and two of every kind of living creature, which He caused to come to Noah for safekeeping on the ark.

It is possible that God left out some of the earth animals, that He didn't cause them to come to Noah, such as the dinosaurs. But the Bible says, "Two of every kind shall come to you to keep them alive."

We can conjecture that either dinosaurs didn't make it onto the ark because, plausibly, God intended them to become extinct at that time, or that because of climatic conditions after the flood, they failed to reproduce in sufficient numbers and died out. We simply don't have enough data to go beyond conjecture at this point.

✚ ADDITIONAL REFERENCE SOURCES

John C. Whitcomb and Henry M. Morris, *The Genesis Flood*, Presbyterian and Reformed Pub. Co., 1961

John C. Whitcomb, *The Early Earth*, Baker Book House, 1972

Do you really believe the story of Jonah and the whale?

Of all the stories in the Bible, the one which people find hardest to swallow is the account of Jonah and the whale. Skeptics have a field day ridiculing the account of a man who was swallowed whole by a whale and lived to tell of it after three days and nights in such surroundings.

In an attempt to avoid the seeming improbabilities of the story, some contend that this story was never meant to be understood literally, but as an allegory. How then does one deal with the story?

The problem of viewing Jonah as an allegory is that the Bible nowhere treats it as such. The story itself is written as a historical narrative, with absolutely no indication that it was intended as myth or allegory.

Second Kings 14:25 refers to Jonah as a historical figure. Jesus Himself treats Jonah as historical, relating that Jonah was a prophet, whose preaching resulted in the people of Nineveh repenting.

He even compared the story to His own death and resurrection: "For just as Jonah was three days and three nights in the belly of the sea-monster, so shall the Son of Man be three days and three nights in the heart of the earth. The men of Nineveh shall stand up with this generation at the judgment, and shall condemn it because they repented at the preaching of Jonah; and, behold, something greater than Jonah is here" (Matthew 12:40, 41, NASB).

If one denies the facts of the story of Jonah, he (or she) must then assume ignorance or deception on the part of Jesus, who believed its authenticity. This would, in effect, destroy His claim to being God.

Having established that Jonah's story was intended to be historical, it is now possible to deal with the problems of his being swallowed by a whale and the three days and nights he is said to have survived within the fish.

The first fact to deal with is that the Hebrew and Greek words which are translated "whale" in the King James Version actually mean "large fish." There are certain species of whales and sharks that are perfectly capable of swallowing a man whole, including the whale shark, white shark, and sperm shark. These giant mammals have been known to swallow whole animals that are larger than man. It could have been a whale that swallowed Jonah, but the Bible was not specific on the species.

The second problem to deal with is Jonah's sojourn within the "great fish." A man named James Bartley is known to have survived a day and a half in the belly of a whale before being rescued. The anatomy of these mammals provides sufficient oxygen for the possibility of survival.

There is also the possibility that Jonah died in the belly of the fish, and that God brought him back to life after three days. This would not be inconsistent with the teaching of Scripture, seeing that at least eight other resuscitations are recorded. However, this is not indicative in the narrative and Jonah could have survived.

✚ ADDITIONAL REFERENCE SOURCES

Henry Morris, *The Bible Has the Answer*, Baker Book House, 1971

Hobart Freeman, *An Introduction to the Old Testament Prophets,* Moody Press, 1969

Gleason Archer, *A Survey of Old Testament Introduction*, rev. ed., Moody Press, 1979

Where did Cain get his wife?

One of the most frequent questions asked by Christians and non-Christians alike is where did Cain's wife come from. This question also involves a larger question: what population existed at the time Cain built his city, and what of incest?

According to Genesis, Cain murdered his younger brother Abel (Genesis 4:8) at some point in his life. As punishment for this crime, God banished Cain from his home and the presence of the Lord.

The Bible also records Cain's fear that others might avenge Abel by killing him (Genesis 4:14), that Cain obtained a wife at some point (Genesis 4:17) and built a city (Genesis 4:17).

One theory that has been put forth to explain the existence of sufficient numbers of people is directly contradictory to Scripture and posits a "pre-Adamic" race dwelling in the neighborhood of the Garden of Eden from which Cain could take a wife.

This is not a tenable solution, however, for the Scriptures clearly teach that Adam was the first man (I Corinthians 15:45) and that his wife, Eve, was "the mother of all the living" (Genesis 3:20, NASB).

Genesis 5:4 tells us that Adam had sons and daughters. At first, sons and daughters of Adam and Eve had to marry each other to populate the earth. Cain probably married a sister or niece or grand niece.

Assuming the accuracy of the Genesis account, and considering the length of lives recorded (around 900 years, on the average), a very sizeable population could have developed very rapidly. Using conservative guesses as to the size of families and average age, there easily could have been several million people living at the time of the death of Cain.

Moreover, the Scriptures nowhere indicate at what points in the life of Cain he murdered his brother, married his wife, or built his city. Even a few hundred years might have passed before all of the events took place, allowing for a sizable population with which to build a city.

All this raises the additional question of incest. If incest is scripturally forbidden, according to the Mosaic law, how do we explain all this marrying of siblings? Since Adam and Eve were created directly by God, and perfect, it can be presumed that their genes were perfect.

When sin entered the world at the Fall, bringing with it death, disease, and destruction, the gene pool would gradually become corrupted. At first, no harm would result from marriage of brothers and sisters, and had sin not entered the world, presumably no harm would have ever entered.

As the generations passed, however, disease, environment, and sin took their toll on the genetic pool, which resulted in mutant and defective genes. Incest was prohibited in Moses' time, from a biological standpoint, because it now was dangerous and resulted in deformed, moronic, or otherwise defective offspring.

Moreover, in addition to the biological problem which arises from incest, there is also an ethical one. God forbids incest on moral grounds, and this is more crucial than the biological aspect (Leviticus 20:11ff).

Incest disrupts the family social and moral structure. The family is the only God-ordained institution in the world other than the church. At the initial formation of the family structure in Cain's day, it is difficult to presume what happened with inter-marriage. Thus we cannot be sure to what extent incest occurred. One thing is certain: after God's ordained family structure stabilized, incest was sin.

✚ ADDITIONAL REFERENCE SOURCES

Henry Morris, *The Bible Has the Answer*, Baker Book House, 1971

H. C. Leupold, *Exposition of Genesis*, Vol. I, Baker Book House, 1958

Does the Bible allow for the theory of evolution?

Q

A This is one of our most often asked questions, and it comes in various forms, such as, "Can a person be a Christian and believe in evolution?" or "Hasn't science proven the theory of evolution, thus contradicting the Genesis account of creation?"

To answer this, we must first understand what we mean by the term evolution. If it is defined as simply "change"—as the development of an infant to an adult or a change within a kind, such as dog or cat—then this would pose no problem. This evolution, or development change within certain kinds, is completely consistent with the Holy Scripture.

The problem is that the prevailing theory of evolution goes far beyond this. The theory states basically that complex elements have developed from simpler elements, and living organisms have sprung from non-living chemicals, by a chance association.

The theory of evolution is less of a scientific theory and more of a philosophy about the origin of life and the meaning of man.

The theory of evolution is contradictory to the biblical narrative of creation. The Genesis account records ten different times how God created plants and animals after their kind with *no* crossing of the kinds. Man was fully man at his creation, as was woman, with no long gradual period of development.

The idea of natural selection, or survival of the fittest, is at odds with the biblical teaching that all things were created good (Genesis 1:31). The Scriptures teach that everything was originally created perfect, and death and decay occurred when sin entered into the universe. This is opposed to the evolutionary concept of everything getting better.

Evolution not only contradicts the Bible, but it also contradicts some basic laws of science. For example, the second law of thermodynamics implies that left to itself, everything tends to become less ordered, not more ordered or "complex."

This rule is an observation of the obvious: things grow old, run down, and eventually die or decay. They lose their structure. The theory of evolution says that things develop their complexity and structure. This is not the case.

Evolution also says that changes or mutations are beneficial, while nature shows almost all variations are harmful. The theory contradicts observable phenomena.

Neither the theory of evolution nor the theory of special creation can be proven scientifically; that is, they cannot be repeated in a laboratory experiment. Special creation happened once in the past, and evolution is too slow to observe.

Both theories are faith assumptions, and on the basis of the evidence one must choose one or the other. The Christian should not be embarrassed for believing the Genesis account of creation, since it not only fits better with observable facts but also was the view of the God-Man Jesus Christ (Matthew 19:1–6).

✚ ADDITIONAL REFERENCE SOURCES

Bolton Davidheiser, *Evolution and the Christian Faith*, Presbyterian and Reformed, 1969

James Coppedge, *Evolution: Possible or Impossible?* Zondervan, 1973

Henry Morris (Ed.), *Scientific Creationism*, San Diego, Christian Life Pub., 1974

Q Were the days in Genesis 1 twenty-four hours or a long period of time?

 Whether the six days of Genesis are solar days as we know them or longer periods of time is a debate with a long history.

Many scientists point to fossils and geological data as proof that the earth is millions of years old, so one of the views held is the age-day theory, which attempts to harmonize the Genesis account with current scientific theory, by holding that the six days were long ages of time, rather than literal days of twenty-four hours.

The arguments used to support the idea that the days were ages of perhaps millions of years are based on the fossil and geological evidence, which are assumed to be accurate as interpreted by evolutionary scientists, and on interpretations of the Genesis account itself.

The supporters of this view, which date back to the earliest Christian era, point out that a twenty-four-hour-day meaning is impossible because the sun isn't recorded as created until the fourth day, so solar days couldn't exist the first three days.

This view also holds that since God is still resting from creation, the seventh day is not a solar day, which means that the others likewise cannot be. Also, the Hebrew word for day, "yom," is used elsewhere in the Bible to indicate longer periods of time than twenty-four hours, such as in Psalms 90:4 and II Peter 3:8; also Zechariah 12–14.

Those who oppose the age-day view point out that the Genesis account doesn't need to be harmonized with science, but that science needs to be harmonized with the Scriptures. The geological and fossil evidence do not conclusively prove an earth age of millions of years, and can in large part be explained by the apparent age theory.

This is the theory that God created everything at full maturity, with the appearance of having gone through the normal development stages. Examples of this would be Adam and Eve, created fully grown, and the wine Jesus created in Cana, fully fermented in an instant of time.

This would explain the earth's appearance of millions of years of age, while in reality it was only recently created (6–20 thousand years ago). Some of the fossil evidence and geological data can also be explained by a universal flood depositing strata and fossils.

Regarding the meaning of "yom," those who oppose the age-day theory point out that when "yom" is used with a specific number, in this case six days, it always means a twenty-four-hour day. Examples of this would be the forty days Moses was on Mt. Sinai and the three days Jonah was inside the great fish.

Additional evidence is that Exodus 20:11 refers to the six days of creation apparently as twenty-four-hour days. More than 700 times in the Old Testament, the plural of "yom" is used and always has twenty-four-hour days in view. The burden of proof is on those who argue that the word "yom" cannot be understood in its plain and natural sense.

As for the argument that the first three days could not be solar days, God could have caused things to operate on the kind of plan He later would use in the solar days, in preparation for the sun's creation on day four.

The Genesis account clearly reports "there was evening and there was morning, one day." Even without the sun, there was an operation like that of the solar days shortly to follow.

While it is true that God is still resting from creation, the Scripture refers to the resting of God in the past tense, not the present. The seventh day does not continue, but was a specific time in the past when He "ceased creating."

Many who oppose the age-day theory hold to a solar day and recent creation view, along with a universal flood and apparent age theory to explain the fossil and geological evidence. As illustrated in this rebuttal to the age-day view, as well as other evidence, there is no compelling reason to abandon the solar day and recent creation view.

Q

But doesn't the Bible contain statements that are at variance with science?

A Non-believers often assert that science has demonstrated the Bible to be outdated. Modern discoveries have (so the arguments go) made laughable the biblical world view. This assertion makes several erroneous assumptions and ignores the perspective of the Bible.

The Bible is not a text book on science. Its purpose is not to explain in technical terms the technical data of the natural world, but to explain God's purpose and relation to man, to deal with spiritual things. It is definitely not a technical textbook for scientists.

The descriptions which the Bible gives concerning nature are neither scientific nor unscientific, but phrased by words that are non-technical and often general, so that even the common reader can follow the thought. This does not at all mean the statements are incorrect; it means that they were written from the viewpoint and in the language of a non-technical observer for readers in general.

Although the Bible was written during a time when many fanciful ideas about the world were prevalent, it shows itself unique in its views of creation, nature, and God. The crude polytheistic account of the Babylonians about the creation of the world is in direct conflict with the sublime record found in the Book of Genesis (cf. the similarities and yet the striking differences that show the superiority of the biblical account in *Archaeology and the Old Testament*, Merrill F. Unger, Grand Rapids, Zondervan, 1954, pp. 26–38).

The prevailing belief of the nations of antiquity is polytheistic, a belief diametrically opposed to the monotheism of the

Bible, the only monotheism in ancient times. The Bible cannot be adequately explained simply as a product of its own environment.

The statements in the Bible concerning scientific matters are on a different level from the other literature of its time. The Scriptures entertain no fanciful ideas of science and of the natural world, but even the learned Greek philosophers had ridiculous notions about light, creation, and astronomy.

The Vedas, which are the Hindu scriptures, teach that "the moon is approximately 150,000 miles higher than the sun and shines with its own light, that the earth is flat and triangular, and that earthquakes are caused by elephants shaking themselves under it!"

It was Ptolemy who suggested that the earth was flat. We read statements such as these and laugh, but there are no absurd statements in the Bible similar to these.

Science and the Scriptures do not cancel each other out. They simply look at the world from different perspectives, but are not finally contradictory.

It makes sense to believe that if the same God created the natural order and also has communicated with men through the Bible, and if He is competent, He would seek to have this twofold witness to Himself *enhance* His cause and not *embarrass* and *discredit* it.

One interesting part to note is that the very origin of modern science rests upon the truth of the Scripture. The fact that there is a God who created and designed an ordered universe prompted men like Newton to search for certain scientific laws to explain this order. So rather than science eroding the foundation of biblical authority, it must find its roots there.

✚ ADDITIONAL REFERENCE SOURCES

Arthur Custance, *Science and Faith*, Zondervan, 1978

Bernard Ramm, *A Christian View of Science and the Scriptures*, Eerdmans, 1966

J. E. Horigan, *Chance or Design?* Philosophical Library, 1979

Henry Morris, *Studies in the Bible and Science*, Baker Book House, 1966

What do you think about various alternatives to Christianity, such as agnosticism, atheism, and humanism?

Many individuals who have rejected the Christian claim have embraced other views of life. Most state that there is no God as the Bible teaches, and if there is, then He is unknowable. The claims of these alternatives will not hold up under investigation.

An agnostic usually is someone who does not know whether God exists. The agnostic has not made up his mind on God. He is a doubter. Some agnostics are more aggressive than others in searching for God, and this we applaud.

The Bible promises, if anyone desires to know the truth about God, they shall. "If any man is willing to do His will, he shall know of the teaching, whether it is of God, or whether I speak from Myself" (John 7:17, NASB).

Unfortunately, most agnostics do not make a real effort to know if there is a God. They do not consider the question all that crucial. Yet it is crucial. The very fact that an agnostic cannot be sure whether there is a God makes it logical that he should consider the claims of Christianity. Therefore, agnosticism is not grounds for rejecting Christianity; rather it is grounds for examining Christianity.

Atheists affirm there is no God. Yet they cannot hold this position dogmatically. For us to be able to make this type of statement with authority, we would have to know the universe in its entirety and to possess all knowledge. If anyone had these credentials, then by definition he would be God.

Thus we see that, unless the atheist is all-knowing, he cannot make a dogmatic statement on God's existence. Therefore, he can only state that he is uncertain whether or not there is a God, and this view is agnosticism. This we have already investigated earlier and found wanting. The atheist's claim that God does not exist crumbles under examination.

The humanist believes that man will be able to solve all his own problems. This creed that "man is the measure of all things" offers no concrete solution to those looking for a way out. Today, in our world, humanism is quite popular.

Humanism fails on two counts. First, man operating by himself cannot set up true standards of justice or values in the world without God. If one man decides his human view of values is correct and another man decides his view is correct, then who will decide between them?

Who would decide between the Nazis and the Jewish race in World War II? Each had a set of values, but who was right? The majority? The nicest? The meanest?

Without a higher standard of authority to go to, which is God, all of life is based on the values of the majority or a dictator in power. They have no sure truth to turn to; it is all a matter of opinion.

Second, humanism believes man is "getting better and better every day in every way." However, with two world wars in this century and the world on the brink of nuclear holocaust, the demise of optimistic humanism is a foregone conclusion.

Thus humanism offers not hope but despair. Humanism does not solve problems; it creates them. If humanism is honestly examined, it leads man not to look to man, but beyond himself, for the answers.

These alternative views, when soundly probed, are found not to undermine Christianity but rather to reinforce it. This is because philosophical systems and other religions, in their search for truth and meaning to life, fall short in their quest. Without the Bible as a solid foundation, there is no way to determine whether or not we have the truth. It alone offers man truth and hope.

✚ ADDITIONAL REFERENCE SOURCES

Francis Schaeffer, *He Is There and He Is Not Silent*, Tyndale House, 1972

E. J. Carnell, *An Introduction to Christian Apologetics,* Eerdmans, 1950

Colin Chapman, *Christianity on Trial*, Tyndale House, 1975

R. C. Sproul, *The Psychology of Atheism*, Bethany Fellowship, 1974

Don't all religions basically teach the same thing?

Many people wonder why we make such a fuss about Jesus Christ and Christianity, since they believe all religions are basically the same. They assume that all faiths are all talking about the same thing, but are putting it in a different way.

One man once gave this illustration. He said, "Suppose you take 10 men and blindfold them, and lead them over to an elephant. You now let each of them touch a different part of the elephant—tail, trunk, etc.—without telling them what they are touching.

"You then lead them back inside, take off their blindfolds and tell them to describe what they touched." The man then asked, "Would their descriptions agree?" The answer of course is no.

The man then made this observation: even though these ten men touched the same thing, they did not agree because each touched a different part or, if you please, experienced it from a different angle. He went on to conclude, "Isn't it the same in the area of religion?

"Aren't all the different religious groups—Christians, Moslems, Mormons, Buddhists, etc.—experiencing the same God, yet explaining it in different ways? Thus can't they all be true, but with each giving a different emphasis?"

The problem with this illustration is identifying the elephant with God. You are assuming that all these people are experiencing the same God, when in fact this is not true. Christianity and Islam cannot both be true at the same time. Neither can Mormonism and Buddhism both be correct simultaneously, nor can Christian Science and Roman Catholicism.

All religions cannot be true at the same time, because they teach many things completely opposite from one another. They all may be wrong, but certainly they all cannot be right, for the claims of one will exclude the other.

As to matters of salvation and the person of Jesus Christ, only historic Christianity recognizes Him as the eternal God becoming a man who died for the sins of the world and arose again the third day. Salvation is obtained only by putting one's trust in this Jesus.

The Jesus of Islam was not the Son of God who died for the sins of the world; neither is the Jesus of Mormonism or Christian Science the same Jesus as revealed in the Bible.

Salvation is not by grace and through faith in these religions, but it is a matter of works. It can then be observed that we are dealing with different religious ideas that are not compatible with one another.

Even though many religions seem to be the same on the surface, the closer one gets to the central teachings the more apparent the differences become. It is totally incorrect to say that all religions are the same.

The God of the Christians is not the same God as that of the Mormons, Moslems, or Christian Scientists. If the God of the Bible is the only true God, then the other gods are non-existent and should not be worshiped.

✚ ADDITIONAL REFERENCE SOURCES

J. N. D. Anderson (Ed.), *The World's Religions*, 4th rev. ed., Eerdmans, 1975

Walter Martin, *The Kingdom of the Cults*, rev. ed., Bethany Fellowship, 1974

Q

What are some of the differences between Christianity and the Eastern religions?

A We are living in a day of increased technology and communication, and by means of such advanced media as television we can witness events as they occur around the globe. This has led to more familiarity with the thoughts and religious beliefs of other people.

East has met West, and we are seeing that there are vast differences between Christianity and the religions of the East.

The God of Eastern thought is impersonal, while the God of the Bible is personal. In some Eastern religions, God is everything and everything is God, while the Bible teaches that God is independent from His creation.

One of the basic concepts of Eastern thought is the concept of material illusion (*maya* in Hindu); the material world is an illusion, and sin is nothing but ignorance about the fact of illusion.

The Scriptures teach that the world has objective reality, and sin, far from being mere ignorance about the illusion of the world, is willful rebellion against the very real, infinite God.

The law of karma is an intricate belief in many of the Eastern religions. Good karma or good works is the way a person will be delivered from the cycle of rebirth, while bad karma will result in a person being reborn in a lower form than the previous life. Salvation is based on works.

The Scriptures teach that human deeds are not even considered in the matters of eternal salvation. "Not by works of righteousness which we have done, but according to his mercy he saved us" (Titus 3:5, KJV). Works do have a very vital place, but they come within the life that has already received the salvation God gives, and are to be the grateful and beautiful expression that salvation for that person is real (Ephesians 2:10).

As for the idea of the transmigration of souls or continuous rebirths until one reaches nirvana or eternal bliss, the Bible teaches no such gospel of the second chance. The teaching of the Scriptures is that each person is unique, not part of everything, and after that unique person dies, he will be accountable to God in judgment (Hebrews 9:27).

The Christian world view is totally different from that in the Eastern religions. History has no purpose or meaning to the Eastern mind; it is a never-ending struggle. The Bible portrays a super-natural God, who is working toward the ultimate goal of setting up His eternal kingdom.

Another avenue which has served to introduce the Western world to Eastern thought is the drug culture. Along with the emphasis on drugs on the university campuses in the 1960s came an emphasis on Eastern religion, which matched perfectly for those looking for a way out. This increased interest in the academic community brought about new literature with Eastern thought forms which then began to permeate our culture. Authors such as Hesse, Casteneda, and Pirsig (*Zen and the Art of Motorcycle Maintenance*) became popular. Even groups such as Transcendental Meditation (T.M.) gained respectability and sprang up everywhere.

There are many other differences between the Eastern religious thought and Christianity; there are few similarities, even of a superficial nature. The above differences are sufficient to indicate the lack of any correspondence between Christianity and Eastern religions on any major, fundamental tenet of belief.

✛ ADDITIONAL REFERENCE SOURCES

Stephen Neill, *Christian Faith and Other Faiths*, Oxford Paperbacks, 1970

J.N.D. Anderson, *Christianity and Comparative Religions*, Inter-Varsity Press, 1971

Kenneth Boa, *Cults, World Religions and You*, Victor Books, 1977

What are the origins of Islam?

Approximately 500 million people, about one-seventh of the world's population, are Moslems. The founder of the religion is Mohammed, who, according to Moslems, was the greatest of all the prophets.

Mohammed was born in A.D. 570 in Mecca. His early years were relatively uneventful as a manager of camel caravans and a keeper of his wife's estate. However, one evening in a cave on Mt. Hira, where he often went to pray, he is said to have heard a loud voice telling him to "read."

Protesting that he could not read, he heard the voice command him again. He was then shown a scroll on which words were emblazoned with fire. Although he had never previously read a word, Mohammed miraculously read the scroll.

He left the cave fearing that he had gone mad, but he heard the voice again. Looking up, Mohammed saw in human form the angel Gabriel, who said to him, "Oh Mohammed! You are Allah's messenger, and I am Gabriel."

This did not yet convince him, the story goes. Later he received another call, which he obeyed. His mission as an apostle of God was to proclaim to his idolatrous people a pure monotheism.

At the outset, his message met with great resistance, which included persecution and exile from his own people. He claimed to receive further revelations from Allah, which proclaimed himself as successor of the prophets, including Noah, Abraham, Moses, and Jesus. Mohammed eventually viewed himself as the final messenger Allah would send to the world, making him *the* prophet.

In A.D. 622, a group of 150 Moslems left Mecca secretly for the town of Yathrib. Mohammed journeyed to Yathrib later that year, on September 20, the date which begins the Moslem calendar. The city was later renamed Medina in honor of Mohammed's eight-year residence there.

At sixty years of age, Mohammed and his army marched upon Mecca in an attempt to claim this as the Holy City of Islam, eventually conquering it against overwhelming odds. Two years later the prophet of Allah died.

The pattern had been set for the followers of Mohammed. The enemies of Allah must be overthrown. Islam quickly spread beyond the Arabian borders, capturing Jerusalem by A.D. 636.

By 715, the empire had spread from the Chinese frontier westward to the Atlantic Ocean. Thus Islam began its quest to follow the principles of Allah, and has subsequently grown into one of the world's major religions.

What are the beliefs of Islam?

As the Jews believed in the Old Testament and the Christians put their faith in both the Old and New Testaments, the Moslems believe the Quran* is the divine word of God. This book, containing the supposed revelations given to Mohammed, is divided into 114 chapters, or Suras. His followers wrote the Quran shortly after Mohammed's death.

To the Moslems, the Quran is God's last word to the world. It states that both the Old and New Testaments are likewise divinely inspired, but have been altered by Christians and Jews. In any place where they conflict, the Bible is wrong and the Quran is correct; the Quran is the final authority (Sura 33:40).

Islam's basic teaching, called the Islamic creed, consists of six basic beliefs, found throughout the Quran. The favorite creed of Islam is, "There is no God but Allah," which is recited daily by the faithful Moslem. The unity of God is a basic tenet of the Moslem faith.

Another cherished belief of the Moslems is the belief in angels as messengers of Allah. That concept in Islam differs little from the biblical view.

Moslems also believe that Allah has revealed himself through Scripture, including the Old Testament, the Gospels (though not believing them to be accurate), the Quran, and the traditions not contained in the Quran called the Hadith. Of the above sources, only the Quran is totally trusted by Moslems.

---

*Quran—commonly called Koran.

Islam also holds a strong belief in the prophets, Mohammed being the greatest since he was sent to the entire world.
Jesus is viewed as a prophet sent only to the Jews.

There is a great emphasis in Islam concerning the Day of
Judgment. All men will be judged according to their works.
Moslems will enter paradise (though some must first be
purged for their sins); non-Moslems will be condemned forever
to a pit of fire.

Besides the five basic beliefs, Muslims also have five pillars
or observances that follow as part of their faith. They are:

1. The creed or statement of belief: "There is no God but
   Allah, and Mohammed is the prophet of Allah."
2. The ritual prayers performed five times a day facing
   Mecca.
3. Alms giving, offering 1/40 of their income for the needy.
4. Their observance of Ramadan where they face during the
   daylight hours.
5. Their pilgrimage to Mecca required of all Muslims before
   death.

There is an unofficial sixth pillar known as the holy war.
This is used to spread Islam.

Finally, Moslems view God as an absolute deity whose will
is law. God is unknowable in the personal sense; thus the goal
of Islam is to obey Allah, not to know him.

Is Islam compatible with Christianity?

As with all world religions, there are tremendous differences between biblical Christianity and Islam. A close examination of the two faiths will find their beliefs to be incompatible.

Mohammed claimed that the revelations given him by God were infallible, thus making the Quran the standard by which the other Scriptures are to be tested. However, the mere claim to revelations is meaningless unless backup up by some kind of adequate evidence.

The evidence for the inspiration and historical reliability of the Bible is overwhelming, while evidence for the infallibility of the Quran is lacking.

Mohammed also asserted that the Gospel portrait of Jesus is incorrect, while the proper view was revealed to him by God. The Moslem thus believes the report in the Quran of the life of Jesus, rather than the New Testament account. The Jesus who is revealed in the Quran is not the same Jesus who is portrayed in the Gospels. Both accounts cannot be true at the same time.

In any event, the teachings of Christianity and Islam cannot be reconciled. The Quran is in direct conflict with the Scriptures on the character of Jesus Christ. "Jesus Christ, the son of Mary, was no more than an apostle of God" (Sura 19:92).

Furthermore, the Quran states that Jesus is a prophet only to the nation Israel, while Mohammed is the last and greatest prophet to the whole world.

Contrast that with the biblical view of Jesus Christ, "In the beginning was the Word, and the Word was with God, and the Word was God" (John 1:1, KJV), "He who has seen me has seen the Father" (John 14:9, RSV), "You are the Christ, the Son of the living God" (Matthew 16:16, MLVB), "And He is the radiance of His glory and the exact representation of His nature, and upholds all things by the word of His power. When He had made purification of sins, He sat down at the right hand of the Majesty on high" (Hebrews 1:3, NASB).

The Quran, speaking of the death of Christ, states, "They neither killed nor crucified him; it had only the appearance of it."

The New Testament, however, makes the mode of Jesus' death very clear: "And when they were come to the place, which is called Calvary, there they crucified him" (Luke 23:33, KJV), "and when Jesus had cried with a loud voice, he said, Father, into Thy hands I commend my spirit: and having said thus, he gave up the ghost" (Luke 23:46, KJV).

The Bible teaches that Jesus was the virgin-born Son of Mary, God in human flesh. "And the angel said to her, 'Do not be afraid, Mary, for you have found favor with God. And behold, you will conceive in your womb and bear a son, and you shall call his name Jesus'" (Luke 1:30, 31, RSV); "And the angel answered and said to her, The Holy Spirit will come upon you and the power of the Most High will overshadow you; therefore that holy Offspring will be called the Son of God'" (Luke 1:35, MLVB).

Islam teaches that Jesus was born miraculously from Mary but they do not believe in the biblical virgin birth. They believe that, as Adam was created from the earth, Jesus was created by God in the womb of Mary. They say He is not a god or the Son of God. Although this would be a miraculous conception, it is not the same as the biblical virgin birth.

Islam also teaches salvation by works: "They whose balances shall be heavy shall be blest. But they whose balances shall be light, they shall lose their soul, abiding in hell forever" (Sura 13:102–140). Thus if the scale tips in favor of good works, the Moslem will reach paradise, but if this be not the case then he will be banished to hell.

The Bible teaches a salvation by grace through faith and not of works. "For by grace you have been saved through faith; and that not of yourselves, it is the gift of God; not as a result of works, that no one should boast" (Ephesians 2:8, 9, NASB), "Not by works of righteousness which we have done, but according to his mercy he saved us" (Titus 3:5, KJV).

A major problem with accepting Mohammed's account is that his testimony is 600 years after the events occurred, while the New Testament contains eyewitness or firsthand testimony of the life and ministry of Jesus Christ. Jesus made the distinction very clear, "This is the work of God, that you believe in him whom he has sent" (John 6:29, RSV).

✚ ADDITIONAL REFERENCE SOURCES

John Elder, *Biblical Approach to the Muslim*, Worldwide Evangelism Crusade,

William M. Miller, *A Christians Response to Islam*, Presbyterian and Reformed, 1976

C. R. Marsh, *Share Your Faith With a Muslim*, Moody Press, 1975

Fazlur Rahman, *Islam*, New York, Anchor Books, 1968

Don McCurry, *The Gospel and Islam*, Monrovia, MARC Publications, 1979

A. J. Arberry, *The Koran Interpreted*, MacMillan Publishing Co., 1964

What makes Christian conversion valid? Can't it be explained psychologically?

Whenever a believer gives his or her testimony, there always seems to be someone who objects to this being used as evidence for the Christian truth-claim. They contend that it seems like everybody has some sort of conversion experience or religious testimony.

The Mormons talk about the burning in their heart; those in Eastern religions will talk about the peace and tranquility they receive; others will admit to a new joy or happiness.

Why is Christian conversion correct and the others incorrect? Can't it be better explained by conditional responses or some type of self-hypnosis?

It is true that many today are testifying to religious experiences in which they claim to have met ultimate reality. At first glance, the Christian sounds like everyone else because he is also claiming to have experienced truth. The unbeliever or casual observer needs more than a mere testimony of subjective experience as a criterion to judge who, if anyone, is right. The difference is that Christians have that criterion.

Christian conversion is linked to the person of Jesus Christ. It is rooted in fact, not wishful thinking. Jesus demonstrated that He had the credentials to be called the unique Son of God. He challenged men and women to put their faith in Him, that they might know God and what life is all about.

Jesus said, "I am come that they might have life, and that they might have it more abundantly" (John 10:10, KJV). When a person puts his faith in Jesus Christ, he enters into personal relationship with God Almighty, which results in changes taking place in his life.

Christian conversion is neither self-improvement nor culturally conditioned. There are many who put their faith in Christ, and do it against the pressures of friends and family. The Christian's experience ultimately depends on God and His work in the person's life. This must take place. The experience is grounded in this fact, not in the person himself.

Besides the fact that Christian conversion is based upon something objective, the resurrection of Christ, there is also the universality of Christian experience that must be considered. From the time of Jesus until today, people from every conceivable background, culture, and intellectual stance have been converted by the person of Jesus Christ.

Some of the vilest individuals who ever walked the face of the earth have become some of the most wonderful saints after trusting Jesus Christ. This must be considered. Because of the diversity of the people, it cannot be explained away simply on the basis of conditioning.

Let's say, for example, that someone approaches you and says that he has found the meaning of life, ultimate reality. He confesses that his life has undergone a drastic change. So you ask him what the key is to this major change. He responds by saying, "Ever since I started wearing a watermelon rind on my head, my life has been changed."

You check with this person's friends, and they tell you that indeed he has been different since the day the rind was put on his head. Now you want to know if this experience is peculiar to this one individual, or if others have made the same claim. Thus you start looking for people with watermelon rinds on their heads.

You look far and wide, but cannot find anyone else with a similar experience. Thus you conclude this person is generating his own experience, and is not meeting ultimate reality.

Christian experience is universal, and though this in and of itself does not make it true, it does make it worth considering. What does make it true is that it is based upon the overwhelming evidence of the deity of Jesus Christ.

✚ ADDITIONAL REFERENCE SOURCES

Josh McDowell, *Evidence That Demands a Verdict*, rev. ed., Here's Life Publishers, 1979

Paul Little, *How To Give Away Your Faith*, Inter-Varsity, 1966

William Barclay, *Turning to God*, Baker, 1964

Norman Geisler, *Philosophy of Religion*, Zondervan, 1974

Q What hope does Christianity offer the world?

A We are living in a day in which people are pessimistic about the future. There have always been pessimists, but now there is a general feeling of hopelessness regarding the future. With the advent of tactical nuclear weapons, fear has engulfed our planet.

Examples of this attitude can be seen in the following statements:

"It is becoming more and more obvious that it is not starvation, not microbes, not cancer, but man himself who is mankind's greatest danger" (Carl Jung, "Epilogue," *Modern Man in Search of a Soul*, New York, Routledge Books, 1933).

"The real problem is in the hearts and minds of men. It is not a problem of physics but of ethics. It is easier to denature plutonium than to denature the evil spirit of man" (Albert Einstein, cited by Mead, p. 192).

"Today, even the survival of humanity is a utopian hope" (Norman O. Brown, *Life Against Death*, London, Sphere Books, Ltd., 1968, p. 267).

"The world has now become too dangerous for anything less than utopia" (John Rader Platt, *The Step to Man*, New York, John Wiley and Sons, Ltd., 1966, p. 196).

The problem of lack of hope and meaning to life is not unique to our generation. It has been expressed by others in the past who have felt the same emptiness as our modern world feels. To a large segment of the population, this life is all that there is, and there is no hope beyond the grave, but this idea is nothing new.

Compare what some of the writers in the past have said concerning death. "Once a man dies, there is no resurrection"

(Aeschylus); "There is hope only for those who are alive, but those who have died are without hope" (Theocritus); "When once our brief light sets, there is one perpetual night through which we must sleep" (Catullus).

Against this background of pessimism, Jesus Christ offers real hope. He gives mankind the opportunity to become right with God and his fellow man. Thus Christianity offers a full life to those who will accept Jesus: "I am come that they might have life, and that they might have it more abundantly" (John 10:10, KJV).

However, the abundant life never ends. There is a hope of life everlasting based upon the promises of God in Jesus Christ. Jesus said, "I am the resurrection, and the life: he that believeth in me, though he were dead, yet shall he live: and whosoever liveth and believeth in me shall never die" (John 11:25, 26, KJV).

In a changing world, there exists an unchanging God whose word lasts forever. "The grass withers, the flower fades: but the word of our God shall stand forever" (Isaiah 40:8, MLB), and He Himself never changes, "Jesus Christ the same yesterday, and today, and forever" (Hebrews 13:8, KJV).

Ralph Barton, one of the top cartoonists of the nation, left this note pinned to his pillow before taking his own life: "I have had few difficulties, many friends, great successes; I have gone from wife to wife, and from house to house, visited great countries of the world, but I am fed up with inventing devices to fill up 24 hours of the day" (Bill Bright, *Jesus and the Intellectual*, p. 14).

Shakespeare commented on life, "It is a tale told by an idiot, full of sound and fury, signifying nothing" (*Tragedy of MacBeth*, V.v.).

What a contrast to the words of the apostle Paul written just before his impending death: "For I am already being poured out as a drink offering, and the time of my departure has come. I have fought the good fight, I have finished the course, I have kept the faith; in the future there is laid up for me the crown of righteousness, which the Lord, the righteous Judge, will award to me on that day; and not only to me, but also to all who have loved His appearing" (II Timothy 4:6–8, NASB).

How do I become a Christian?

 "As the kings of the earth and the mighty men of the earth are born in exactly the same way physically as the simplest men, so the most intellectual person must become a Christian in exactly the same way as the simplest person.

"This is true for all men everywhere, through all space and all time. There are no exceptions. Jesus said in a totally exclusive word: 'No man cometh unto the Father, but by me'" (John 14:6, KJV) (Francis Schaeffer, *True Spirituality*, p. 1).

Jesus said that to enter the kingdom of heaven a person must be "born again" (John 3:3). This consists of an act of the heart in believing in Jesus Christ as Lord and Savior. When we were born into the world physically, we were born spiritually dead, and therefore we need a spiritual birth. The spiritual birth involves two facets.

The first is to realize that we cannot make it on our own. We are sinners who need help. What is a sinner? A sinner is someone who is separated from God, has chosen to go his own way and cannot get back to God on his own because of his sin.

Sin can be simply characterized as our own self-centered pride and selfishness. More specifically, sin is the violation of a holy God's standard of righteousness.

Thus, we must own up to the fact that we need a Savior, someone who will accomplish all that God requires. The only person ever to do this was Jesus Christ. He lived the only life that was acceptable to God.

He died as a substitute on the cross for our sins, because we have no chance of pleasing God on our own merit. Thus the initial step is to realize that we all have sinned, broken God's law and deserve judgment as a result. The Bible says, "The wages of sin is death" (Romans 6:23, KJV).

Once a person sees his hopeless condition and realizes that Jesus Christ offers an answer, the next step is to receive that offer personally, for "the gift of God is eternal life through Jesus Christ our Lord" (Romans 6:23, KJV). When a person receives Christ as his Savior by accepting God's gift, at that moment he becomes born again.

It is so easy a child can do it, but it is hard because we first have to realize that we cannot do it on our own. Jesus said to enter the kingdom of heaven, a person must be willing to humble himself as a child, and only then will God receive him (Matthew 18:3).

How about you? Have you done this? Have you been born again? If you wish to do it, we offer this prayer that you might pray: "Lord Jesus, I know that I'm a sinner; I realize that I can't make it on my own. Thank You for dying for me. Right at this moment, the best way I know how, I trust You as my Savior and Lord, in Jesus' name. Amen."

If you prayed sincerely to God, then you have become a Christian! We would encourage you to write to the address at the front of this book for help in your new life.

One thing which is important to note, though, is that it is not the reciting of the above words which makes the difference. There is nothing magical in them; anyone can repeat a sentence. It is the attitude of your heart and your desire when you pray and trust Christ that makes the difference.

If you are still doubtful how this all applies to you, turn right now to page 210.

Is Christianity a crutch?

Every single college, it seems, has the campus atheist who says, "Christianity is for the weaklings; it is just a crutch."

Karl Marx's famous line, "Religion is the opiate of the masses," is still a common view of many. Those who call themselves Christians are seen as people who need something to enable them to cope with the problems of life. Some people use alcohol, some drugs, others Christianity to get themselves through this difficult world.

The fact of the matter is we all *do* need a crutch to get by in this world. We are all crippled in some sense, and down deep inside there is a desire for something to sustain us. The real issue is, "Is this crutch we call Christianity true, or is it something on the same level as drugs or alcohol, invented to meet an admitted need?"

There are definite psychological needs, fear of danger, disease, and death, that might prompt us to invent God so that we would feel secure. However, there are also psychological needs that might lead us to deny that God exists. The agnostic or atheist may be using his agnosticism or atheism as a crutch to avoid the responsibility of God's demands.

The God of the Bible is awesome and a threat to mankind. A God who is all-powerful, all-knowing, righteous, holy, and just, and who is going to judge the world for its sin, is an extremely imposing figure. Thus it is only fair to point out that some need the crutch of denying God's existence in order to live their lives as they please without fear of judgment.

Aldous Huxley articulated this in *Ends and Means*: "For myself, the philosophy of meaningless was essentially an instrument of liberation, sexual and political" (*Ends and Means*, p. 270 ff.).

The truth of the Christian faith is not based upon psychological needs for or against God. Yes, it is possible that Christianity could have started because people need something to lean on, but the question is not how it *could* have started but how it *did* start.

We again are brought back to the real issue, which is the person of Jesus Christ. Does mankind need to lean on Him, or can we lean on something else?

Jesus made the issue very clear, "Therefore whosoever heareth these sayings of mine, and doeth them, I will liken him unto a wise man, which built his house upon a rock: and the rain descended, and the floods came, and the winds blew, and beat upon that house; and it fell not: for it was founded upon a rock.

"And every one that heareth these sayings of mine, and doeth them not, shall be likened unto a foolish man, which built his house upon the sand: and the rain descended, and the floods came, and the winds blew, and beat upon that house; and it fell: and great was the fall of it." (Matthew 7:24–27, KJV).

One could also state it this way. A crutch presupposes two things: (1) that there is a disease, sickness, or hurt, and (2) that a person has been given some type of a remedy (this is why he has the crutch).

Two questions immediately arise. First, what is this disease? Is it real or imagined? And second, is the remedy the correct one for the disease?

With Christianity, God clearly states that the disease is sin, and that the disease is real. It is not a psychological, imaginary hand-up in need of a religious fix as Marx would propound. Rather, the remedy instead of being a religious crutch, is a relationship with Jesus Christ.

Therefore, Christianity in one sense is a crutch. But it is more than a crutch; it is the sure foundation, the truth of life.

If Jesus Christ be God and died on the cross for our sins and created us to be in fellowship with God the Father through Him, then to call Him a crutch would be like a light bulb saying to an electrical socket, "You are my crutch." As a light bulb was created to function properly when inserted into the socket, so we have been created to function properly in a personal relationship with God through Jesus Christ.

Q

Why should I become a Christian? The worst hypocrites are in church.

A

One major excuse that people use in their refusal to embrace Christianity concerns hypocrites in the Church, both past and present. People like to point to past misdeeds done in the name of Christ, such as the Spanish Inquisition, witch trials, and other horrible acts.

Then, there are the present-day examples of preachers, deacons, or church leaders who have been caught in alcoholism, adulterous relationships, or some other inconsistency with what they say they believe. This type of behavior has led many to say, "If that's what Christianity is all about, then I don't want any part of it."

It must be admitted that there has been hypocrisy in the Church, and today we are not exempt from people who are hypocritical. A hypocrite is an actor, one who puts on a false face. He says one thing but does another.

However, just because the Church contains hypocrites does not mean that all Christians are hypocrites. With every example of hypocrisy that can be pointed to in the Church, a counter example can be pointed out showing people who are living consistently with the teaching of Jesus Christ.

It is important not to confuse hypocrisy with sin. All Christians are sinners, but not all Christians are hypocrites. There is a misconception that a Christian is a person who claims that he does not sin, but the truth is that to call oneself a Christian is to admit to being a sinner (I John 1:5–2:2).

All believers, including the clergy, are fallible human beings who are prone to all types of sin. Just because a person is not perfect does not mean that he is a phony. The distinction between the two is important. The failures of the believers do not invalidate the truth.

Jesus Christ had very harsh words for people who were committing the sin of hypocrisy, especially the religious leaders of His day. He denounced them in no uncertain terms.

"Woe unto you, scribes and Pharisees, hypocrites! for ye compass sea and land to make one proselyte, and when he is made, ye make him twofold more the child of hell than yourselves" (Matthew 23:15, KJV).

People can and do enter the ministry for the wrong reasons, or they can compromise the convictions of the faith. When people do this they are wrong, and the Bible denounces this clearly.

Christianity does not stand or fall on the way Christians have acted throughout history or are acting today. Christianity stands or falls on the person of Jesus, and Jesus was not a hypocrite. He lived consistently with what He taught, and at the end of His life He challenged those who had lived with Him night and day, for over three years, to point out any hypocrisy in Him.

His disciples were silent, because there was none. Since Christianity depends on Jesus, it is incorrect to try to invalidate the Christian faith by pointing to horrible things done in the name of Christianity.

The non-believer cannot be excused from believing just because it is possible to point to those who simply pretend to be what they are not. Hypocritical Christians cannot be excused on the basis of not being perfect because of the terrible effects hypocrisy has.

Let's look at one illustration of the reasoning involved in this question. For example, let's say the president of a large car company is always advertising and telling his friends that a certain make of car in his company is the best in the country and the only car we should be driving.

In fact, a number of automotive magazines and consumer groups have backed up some of his claims. But yet, when you see this man, he is driving the competition's leading model! (Perhaps he likes their colors better.)

You say, what a hypocrite! If he believed all that stuff about his car, and he's in a position to know, then he'd be driving one. That is probably true. Yet his being a hypocrite does *not* invalidate the claim that his car may be the best one in the country.

The same is true of Christianity. People may claim it's true, yet have lives inconsistent with their claim, but this does not necessarily mean Christianity is not true.

What about those who have never heard?

No matter where we go or what subject we are speaking on, this question always seems to come up. Many times it is asked to relieve the individual of any personal responsibility to God.

It must be kept in mind, however, that the answer to this question does not determine whether Christianity is true or not. That matter has already been solved in Jesus Christ by His resurrection from the dead. The matter of authority has been solved once and for all, and this issue of those who haven't heard is now merely a matter of interpretation.

The best way to deal with this question is to state certain truths that the Scripture make very plain. The Bible is very clear that no one can come to God except through Jesus Christ.

Jesus said, "No one comes to the Father except through Me" (John 14:6, MLB). The only basis for forgiveness of sin and life everlasting is the way made by Jesus. Many people think this implies that those who have never heard about Jesus will be automatically damned. However, we do not know this is the case.

Although the Scriptures never explicitly teach that someone who has never heard of Jesus can be saved, we do believe that it infers this. We do believe that every person will have an opportunity to repent, and that God will not exclude anyone because he happened to be born at the wrong place and at the wrong time.

Jesus said, "If any man will do his will, he shall know of the doctrine, whether it be of God, or whether I speak of myself" (John 7:17, KJV).

The Bible also reveals that no one has any excuse. "For what can be known about God is plain to them, because God has shown it to them. Ever since the creation of the world his invisible nature, namely, his eternal power and deity, has been clearly perceived in the things that have been made. So they are without excuse" (Romans 1:19–20, RSV).

It is a fact that all of mankind can tell that a creator does exist, because His creation testifies to it. This testimony is universal. Although the people have enough information that God does exist, they become wilfully ignorant of the things of God because their hearts are evil.

The Bible teaches that the unbelieving individual is "holding down the truth in unrighteousness" (Romans 1:18, Lit. Trans). Moreover, the Scriptures relate that man is not seeking after God but actually running from Him. "There is none that seeketh after God" (Romans 3:11, KJV). Therefore, it is not a case of God refusing to get His Word to someone who is desperately searching for the truth.

We also know that it is God's desire that none "should perish but that all should come to repentance" (II Peter 3:9, KJV). This indicates that God also cares for those persons who have not heard the gospel. He has demonstrated this by sending His Son to die in their place. "While we were yet sinners, Christ died for us" (Romans 5:8, KJV).

The Bible teaches that God is going to judge the world fairly and righteously. "Because he hath appointed a day, in which he will judge the world in righteousness" (Acts 17:31, KJV). This means that when all the facts are in, God's name will be vindicated and no one will be able to accuse Him of unfairness.

Even though we may not know how He is going to deal with these people specifically, we know that His judgment is going to be fair. Just this fact alone should satisfy anyone who wonders how God is going to deal with people who have never heard of Jesus Christ.

The Bible itself testifies to the fact that there are those who will hear and respond out of every people on the earth. "For you were killed, and have redeemed us to God by your blood out of every kindred, and tongue, and people, and nation" (Revelation 5:9).

The Bible gives an example of a man who was in a situation not unlike many today. His name was Cornelius. He was a very religious man who was constantly praying to God. He had not heard of Jesus Christ, but he was honestly asking God to reveal Himself to him.

God answered the prayer of Cornelius, and sent the apostle Peter to him to give him the full story of Jesus. When Peter preached to him, Cornelius put his trust in Christ as his Savior. This example demonstrates that anyone who is sincerely desiring to know God will hear about Jesus.

There are people today, like Cornelius, who are praying the same prayer to know the true and living God, and they are being reached no matter where they might live. Simon Peter stated, "I perceive that God is no respecter of persons: But in every nation he that feareth him, and worketh righteousness, is accepted with him" (Acts 10:34–35, KJV).

The Scriptures contain other examples of individuals who were accepted by God, even though their knowledge of Him was limited. Rahab, the prostitute, had only the smallest amount of knowledge of God, but the Bible refers to her as a woman of faith, and her actions were commended (Joshua 2:9; Hebrews 11:31).

Naaman, the Syrian, was granted peace with God because he exercised faith, even though he was living in the midst of a pagan culture (II Kings 5:15–19). Jonah, the prophet, was sent to Nineveh, a heathen society, and they repented at his preaching (Jonah 3:5).

No one will be condemned for not ever hearing of Jesus Christ. That person will be condemned for violating his own moral standard. "For as many as have sinned without law shall also perish without law: and as many as have sinned in the law shall be judged by the law; (For not the hearers of the law are just before God, but the doers of the law shall be justified.

"For when the Gentiles, which have not the law, do by nature the things contained in the law, these, having not the law, are a law unto themselves: Which shew the work of the law written in their hearts, their conscience also bearing witness, and their thoughts the mean while accusing or else excusing one another;) In the day when God shall judge the secrets of men by Jesus Christ according to my gospel" (Romans 2:12–16, KJV).

Based on the above examples from Scripture, it can be seen that God will fairly judge all mankind and that no one can claim that he or she received an unfair hearing. Therefore, the people who ask this question should be very careful not to use this as an excuse for not coming to Christ.

What you think might happen or might not happen to someone else does not relieve your responsibility on Judgment Day. Although we might not be able to answer the question about those who haven't heard to the satisfaction of everyone, there are certain things that the Bible has made clear.

One person put it this way, "Many things in the Bible I cannot understand; many things in the Bible I only think I understand; but there are many things in the Bible I cannot misunderstand" (Anonymous).

✚ ADDITIONAL REFERENCE SOURCES

Josh McDowell, "Romans—The Revolutionary Revelation," 8-Tape series, Liberation Tapes, P.O. Box 6044, Lubbock, Texas 79413

Don Stewart, "What's Going To Happen to Those Who Haven't Heard?" (tape) The Word for Today, P.O. Box 8000, Costa Mesa, CA 92626

R. C. Sproul, *Objections Answered*, G/L Publications, Regal Books, 1978

Paul Little, *How To Give Away Your Faith*, Inter-Varsity Press, 1966

Norman Geisler, *The Roots of Evil*, Zondervan/Probe Ministries, 1978

Q *I know people who are very religious and totally sincere, but not Christians. God will accept them, won't He?*

A A person can be sincere, but he also can be sincerely wrong. The Bible says there is a way that seems right to a man, but the end of this is the way of death (Proverbs 16:25).

There are many cases each year when someone jokingly points a gun at someone else, sincerely believing it is empty. The gun goes off and the other individual is killed, with the person pulling the trigger saying, "I didn't know it was loaded."

That person might be 100% sincere in the fact that he did not want to harm the other individual, but he was sincerely believing something that just was not true. Sincerity is not enough, if the object of belief is not true, and all the sincerity in the world will not bring that person who has been shot with the gun back to life.

The apostle Paul teaches that simply practicing religion does not excuse anyone, but rather it may compound the person's guilt. In examining the pagan's religion, Paul points out that it is a distortion of the truth. He says, "They exchanged the truth of God for a lie" (Romans 1:25, NASB).

The glory of God is substituted and replaced by the glory of the creature. Their religion is one of idolatry, and to worship idols is an insult to the dignity of God. This is something God has always detested.

"You shall have no other gods before Me. You shall not make for yourself an idol, or any likeness of what is in heaven above or on the earth beneath or in the water under the earth. You shall not worship them or serve them; for I, the Lord your

God, am a jealous God" (Exodus 20:3–5, NASB). Thus a religious person has no advantage if he is worshiping the wrong God, no matter how sincere.

If a person attempts to get into a movie theater and the price is $4, it does not matter whether he has $3.90 or 25¢; he is still short. If someone is believing the wrong thing, it does not matter how sincere he is, for he is short of what God requires of men to reach Him.

God sets the standard, and He will accept only those who come to Him through Jesus Christ. "Neither is there salvation in any other: for there is none other name under heaven given among men, whereby we must be saved" (Acts 4:12, KJV).

✚　ADDITIONAL REFERENCE SOURCES

John Warwick Montgomery, *How Do We Know There Is a God?* Bethany Fellowship, 1972

R. C. Sproul, *Objections Answered,* G/L Publications, Regal Books, 1978

If Christianity is so great, why are there so few Christians?

Christians are now and have always been in the minority. Most of the people presently living have not trusted Jesus Christ as their Savior. This, however, is exactly as Jesus said it would be. "Strait is the gate, and narrow is the way, which leadeth unto life, and few there be that find it" (Matthew 7:14, KJV). This has been the case throughout all of history. There are several reasons why a large part of humanity has rejected Jesus as their Savior.

One reason people do not become Christians is out of ignorance. This is not ignorance that there is a God or a person named Jesus Christ, but rather ignorance to the facts validating the Christian faith. Many times this ignorance is self-imposed. Some people are not even bothering to consider the claims of Christ, while others are actively refusing to believe.

Many people claim they have intellectual problems with the Christian faith, when usually what they have are intellectual or emotional excuses. We are aware of many people who, after having been presented the facts of Christianity, have readily admitted that they know Christianity is true, yet they still refuse to become Christians.

This, therefore, is not a problem of the mind, but of the will. It is not that they cannot become Christians; it is more of a matter that they will not become Christians. The Bible teaches that humanity is attempting to suppress the truth of God (Romans 1:18). People are ignorant of the credentials of Jesus, by and large, because they want to be.

Another reason is the simplicity of the gospel. It is so simple to become a Christian that even a child can do it. In fact, to enter the kingdom of heaven, Jesus taught that we must become as children (Matthew 18:3). In simple faith, we must place our trust in Christ whether we be college professors or people who have never finished grammar school.

The apostle Paul said concerning the simplicity of the gospel, "For ye see your calling, brethren, how that not many wise men after the flesh, not many mighty, not many noble, are called: But God hath chosen the foolish things of the world to confound the wise; and God hath chosen the weak things of the world to confound the things which are mighty . . . That no flesh should glory in his presence" (I Corinthians 1:26, 27, 29, KJV).

Paul taught, as did Jesus, that Christians would never be in the majority, and that not many prominent people would believe in Jesus. Although there have not been many great men and women in history who have trusted Jesus, there have been some.

Further, people don't become Christians because of the mistaken idea of what really is a Christian. Many think Christianity is a religion with a set of negative commandments saying, "Don't do this or don't do that." They get the idea that, when you believe in Jesus, you resign yourself to a life of unhappiness, restrictions, and boredom.

Since no one wants to live that way, they write off Christianity as something to which they don't want to commit their lives. It is a sad fact that some Christians give the impression to the world that their faith consists only of a group of negative commandments. Nothing could be further from the truth.

When a person trusts Jesus as Saviour, he becomes truly free. Jesus said, "If the Son therefore shall make you free, ye shall be free indeed" (John 8:36, KJV). Jesus Christ is in the business of setting men and women free from things that have them in bondage so that they can be the type of people they were meant to be.

As believers, we are free to do what we want to do and not do what we don't want to do. The Christian life is anything but boring, because there is the daily joy and excitement of knowing the living God and experiencing all the good things He has in store for us. "Delight thyself also in the Lord; and he shall give thee the desires of thine heart" (Psalms 37:4, KJV).

Some people don't become Christians because of guilt feelings. They have lives in which they've committed many ugly acts and crimes, and they don't believe they can be forgiven by God and that a decent life can be given to them. However, the Bible clearly teaches that anyone, without exception, who seeks God and desires to be forgiven of his sins will be forgiven.

There is no sin that's too great to stop someone from going to heaven except the sin of unbelief. If a person refuses to believe in God's provision for his sin—the person of Jesus Christ—then there is no hope for him. Jesus said, "Him that cometh to me I will in no wise cast out" (John 6:37, KJV).

The Bible says, "For God so loved the world, that he gave his only begotten Son, that whosoever believeth in him should not perish, but have everlasting life" (John 3:16, KJV). You and I are included in that "whosoever." If you will come to Jesus, He has promised to forgive you of your sins, and He will allow you to start over again with a clean slate, no matter how corrupt you have been.

Another reason some refuse to accept Jesus is because of some specific sin in their life. They realize that, if they become a believer, they will have to stop committing that certain sin, and they do not want to stop. Jesus said, "And this is the condemnation, that light is come into the world, and men loved darkness rather than light, because their deeds were evil" (John 3:19, KJV).

Many people love their sin to the point that they will miss getting to heaven. To become a Christian, a person must repent (change his heart and mind) of his sins, and this many people are not willing to do even though Jesus said, "Except ye repent, ye shall all likewise perish" (Luke 13:3, KJV).

In addition, people refuse to believe in Jesus because of self-centeredness. Someone has said—correctly, we believe— that Christianity is the *easiest* religion in the world to believe, and it is also the *most difficult* religion in the world to believe.

It is the easiest because God has done everything for us that needs to be done, and it is impossible to add to the work of Christ. It is the most difficult because we have to admit to ourselves and to God that we cannot do anything to save ourselves.

Our pride does not like that, since we want to work out our own salvation our way. Human nature desires that we dictate our own terms, but God will accept us only on His terms, and this fact keeps many people out of the kingdom.

There are many reasons why people reject Christ, but there are no good reasons.

✛ ADDITIONAL REFERENCE SOURCES

Josh McDowell, "Evidence for Faith" (7-tape series), Liberation Tapes, P.O. Box 6044, Lubbock, Texas 79413

Is it sensible to believe in Christianity or is it just a matter of wishful thinking?

James Harvey Johnson of the Thinkers Club put it this way:

"Religious beliefs are against common sense. There are no angels, devils, heavens, hells, ghosts, witches, nor miracles. These superstitious beliefs are promoted for the purpose of making the gullible believe that by paying money to the priest class they will be favored by one of the gods. There is nothing supernatural—nothing contrary to natural law" (*Religion Is A Gigantic Fraud*, San Diego, CA: The Thinkers Club, Box 2832, Dept. RG).

Often the believer is accused of "assassinating his brains" because he believes in the inspiration of the Bible, miracles, and the resurrection of Jesus Christ. People assume that the Christian belief is based upon ignorance, and that faith is something that is blind and unintelligent.

In reality it is just the opposite. The Christian faith is an intelligent faith; it never consists of a mindless act which is unrelated to reality. The Bible encourages both the believer and the non-believer to use their minds when investigating Christianity.

Jesus said, "You shall love the Lord your God with all your heart, and with all your soul, and with all your mind" (Matthew 22:37, RSV). The apostle Paul told Timothy, "I know whom I have believed" (II Timothy 1:12, KJV) and he told a group of believers in Thessalonica to "prove all things; hold fast that which is good" (I Thessalonians 5:21, KJV).

John, the evangelist, warned people to "try the spirits whether they are of God" (I John 4:1, KJV). This involves using your mind rather extensively.

Further references illustrate the necessity of using one's mind with regard to Christian faith.

"And when Jesus saw that he had answered *intelligently*, He said to him, 'You are not far from the kingdom of God'" (Mark 12:34, NASB).

"Now Jesus did many other signs in the presence of the disciples, which are not written in this book; but these are written that you may believe that Jesus is the Christ, the Son of God, and that believing you may have life in his name" (John 20:30, 31, RSV).

"To whom also he shewed himself alive after his passion by many infallible proofs, being seen of them forty days, and speaking of the things pertaining to the kingdom of God" (Acts 1:3, KJV).

"And this I pray, that your love may abound yet more and more in *knowledge* and in all *judgment*; that ye may approve things that are excellent (discern); that ye may be sincere and without offense till the day of Christ" (Philippians 1:9, 10, KJV).

"That the God of our Lord Jesus Christ, the Father of glory, may give to you a spirit of wisdom and of revelation in the knowledge of Him. I pray that the eyes of your heart may be enlightened, so that you may know what is the hope of His calling, what are the riches of the glory of His inheritance in the saints" (Ephesians 1:17, 18, NASB).

"I speak as to sensible men; judge for yourselves what I say" (I Corinthians 10:15, RSV).

Nothing in Scripture indicates that faith is equal to foolishness, and much indicates the opposite. "Thou shalt not think" is *not* one of the Ten Commandments.

In the Old Testament, God showed respect for man's intellectual integrity. He performed a miracle through Moses and Aaron to demonstrate to Pharaoh their divine mission (Exodus 7:9). He told the Israelites to ignore any prophet who gave false predictions (Deuteronomy 18:22).

He challenged the idols to prove that they were gods. "Set forth your case, says the Lord; bring your proofs. . . . Tell us what is to come hereafter, . . . that we may be dismayed and terrified" (Isaiah 41:21–23, RSV).

And because the idols didn't perform, God said, "Behold, you are nothing, and your work is nought; an abomination is he who chooses you" (Isaiah 41:24, RSV).

Many people who are Christians don't know why they believe in Jesus, even though the Scriptures make it clear that they should know. "Be ready always to give an answer to every man that asketh you a reason of the hope that is in you" (I Peter 3:15, KJV).

This fact doesn't invalidate the Christian faith; it just points out that there are ignorant Christians. Although some Christians haven't thought out why they believe, it is no reflection on the truth of Christianity. The issue is Jesus Christ, not the ignorance of someone who is a believer.

We have seen that the Bible exhorts us to use our minds in making decisions about Jesus Christ. Christianity is sensible; it is reasonable, but one does not come to Jesus with the mind alone. Faith must be exercised, yet the faith is based upon facts, not false hope.

Today people picture Christian faith as a blind leap into the dark, when it actually is a step towards the light. The apostle Paul, while defending the Christian faith before an unbelieving king, said, "For the king knoweth of these things, before whom also I speak freely: for I am persuaded that none of these things are hidden from him; for this thing was not done in a corner" (Acts 26:26, KJV).

The facts about Jesus were well known to this king, along with the other people living at that time. They could be weighed and evaluated by anyone who desired to investigate their validity. The miracles of Jesus occurred in full view of the public, and because of this the early Christians challenged the world to see for themselves "if these things be so."

They didn't discourage the people who were skeptical by saying, "Just believe." They encouraged their curiosity to check out the foundations of the Christian faith (Acts 17:11).

The faith of the Christian is not only open to verification, but it is also subject to falsification. The non-Christian is encouraged to use his mind to check out the claims of Jesus Christ. If some valid evidence would come to light which would really undermine Christianity, such as disproving the resurrection, then the Christian faith would crumble.

Many people have attempted to do this—in e.g., the lawyer, Frank Morrison, and General Lew Wallace, author of *Ben Hur*—and have wound up becoming Christians. The challenge to refute the Christian faith has been laid out many times, but it has never been successfully followed through.

If it is mere "blind faith" that the Christian exercises, why are so many learned men and women still becoming believers by way of the exercise of their intellects? The faith is still standing up to the test because it is based upon truth. "Jesus saith unto him, I am the . . . truth" (John 14:6, KJV).

The choice to become a Christian should be made after proper reflection. It should be considered and evaluated before a commitment is made. A person needs to understand what he is doing before he becomes a Christian. Those who encourage conversion through Jesus Christ, based upon an emotional appeal or through some process of manipulation, are not being biblical.

We are sure that in the long run it will take more faith *not* to believe, if one will give an adequate hearing to the facts. The evidence speaks loudly and clearly to anyone willing to be intellectually honest about the issue of who Jesus Christ truly is. If anyone gives a fair hearing, it will be "blind faith" to reject the claims that are testified to "by many infallible proofs" (Acts 1:3, KJV).

✚ ADDITIONAL REFERENCE SOURCES

John Warwick Montgomery, "Sensible Christianity" (tape series), Christian Research, P.O. Box 500, San Juan Capistrano, Calif. 92693

Josh McDowell, "Evidence for Faith" (tape series), Liberation Tapes

C. S. Lewis, *Mere Christianity*, New York, MacMillan, 1953

John Warwick Montgomery, *Faith Founded on Fact*, Thomas Nelson Publishers, 1978

J. N. D. Anderson, *A Lawyer Among Theologians*, Eerdmans, 1974

Irwin H. Linton, *A Lawyer Examines the Bible*, Boston, W.A. Wilde Co., 1943

Simon Greenleaf, *Testimony of the Evangelists by the Rules of Evidence Administered in Courts of Justice*, Baker Book House, 1965, reprint

Don't my good works count for anything? Will not God accept me if I've lived a good life?

In the early sixties, a song came out by J. Frank Wilson and the Cavaliers, entitled "The Last Kiss." The song is about a couple out on a date who get into a car accident. The girl dies in her boyfriend's arms. He mourns her death singing:

"Oh, where, oh where, can my baby be,/The Lord took her away from me,/She's gone to heaven so I got to be good,/So I can see my baby when I leave this world."

This song sums up the attitude of a lot of people. They think if they can live a good life, if the good works they do outweigh the bad, then they will have earned their way to heaven.

Unfortunately, the Bible does not allow anyone to earn his way to heaven. The Scriptures teach that good works have nothing to do with one entering into a right relationship with God. This relationship is nothing we can earn, because God has done everything for us.

"Not by works of righteousness which we have done, but according to his mercy he saved us" (Titus 3:5, KJV).

"For by grace are ye saved through faith; and that not of yourselves: it is the gift of God: Not of works, lest any man should boast" (Ephesians 2:8, 9, KJV).

"But without faith it is impossible to please him" (Hebrews 11:6, KJV).

"This is the work of God, that ye believe on him whom he hath sent" (John 6:29, KJV).

If our eternal salvation was on the basis of works and we could earn it successfully, then God would be our debtor: He would owe us something (Romans 4:1–3). The Bible teaches that God owes no man anything, and our own righteousness is as filthy rags (Isaiah 64:6).

The simple reason is that God has a perfect standard, and all of us have sinned and come short of this mark (Romans 3:23). We like to compare ourselves to others, and thus we feel that we are not so bad after all. But God compares us to Jesus Christ, and next to Him we cannot help but fall far short, all of us without exception.

This can be illustrated by the following example. Out in Southern California, there is an island off the coast called Catalina, twenty-six miles from the pier at Newport Beach. Suppose that one day three men are standing on the end of the pier.

One is an alcoholic, grubby, sick, living in the streets. The second is the average American, and the third a fine, upstanding, pillar-of-the-community person.

All of a sudden, the alcoholic leaps off the edge of the pier five feet out into the water. The other two yell, "What are you trying to do?" The man in the water yells back, "I'm jumping to Catalina!"

The second man, the average man on the street, says, "Watch me. I can do better than that!" He proceeds to jump, landing ten feet out, twice as far as the alcoholic. The third man, very moral, upright, outstanding person that he is, laughs disdainfully at the two men in the water.

He moves back about fifty yards, takes a running leap and lands twenty feet out, twice as far as Mr. Average, and four times as far as Mr. Alcoholic.

The Coast Guard fishes them out of the water and asks what they are doing, to which they all reply, "We are jumping to Catalina," and Mr. Average boasts of his beating Mr. Alcoholic, and Mr. Great boasts of his accomplishment in beating both of them.

The Coast Guard officer could only shake his head and exclaim, "You fools! You are all *still* twenty-six miles short of your mark."

Although modern man considers himself better than—or at least as good as—others, he is still far from the target God has set for us. It is impossible for anyone to jump from the pier to Catalina, and it is impossible for anyone to reach heaven by his own deeds and apart from Jesus Christ. As Jesus Himself puts it, "No man cometh unto the Father, but by Me" (John 14:6, KJV).

Can Christianity be proved?

Many times during conversations relating to truth, particularly religious truth, someone asks the question, "Can you *prove* Christianity to be true?" Most often, however, the question is phrased, "Can you say *100% for certain* that Christianity is true?"

The answer to the first question is, "Yes, Christianity can be proven to be true." This, of course, does not mean that everyone will *accept* the evidence, however good it is. But the answer to the second question is, "No, not 100% for certain."

Some people feel that this "no" lets them off the hook. The problem is a misunderstanding of the nature of proof. The key is *not* a perfect or absolute certainty, as some believe, but a standard of proof that amounts to a moral certainty or puts the matter beyond a reasonable doubt.

This is the standard used in our courts of law historically. When a judge charges a jury, he or she tells them to decide based on probability, not certainty; based on the evidence presented, not the certainty of having viewed the crime. If jury decisions were delayed until 100% certainty existed, no verdict would ever be rendered.

Everybody makes the decisions of life based on probability, not certainty. Decisions are based on a combination of faith related to fact. For example, a person about to cross a road stands on one side, looks both directions (hopefully he does!), collecting the evidence necessary to determine the probability of making the journey across in safety.

He can never be 100% certain that he will make it. He could have a heart attack halfway across, an earthquake could swallow him, etc. The lack of 100% certainty doesn't keep him on the side of the road, however. He moves out toward the other side with maybe 90% certainty and 10% faith, but he must take himself 100% across.

Many people seem to demand absolute certainty in religious matters, when they don't apply the standard of absolute certainty to anything else of major importance. The atheist cannot even be 100% certain of his belief, "There is no God."

To deny the existence of God necessitates admitting the possibility of His existence. People do not stop making decisions because they cannot reach absolute certainty. A high standard of proof is needed, but not an unreasonable one, like the demand for 100% certainty.

Just as the man crossing the street didn't need 100% certainty to take those steps across, neither does anyone need 100% certainty to make a decision to believe in Christianity, in Jesus Christ.

Christianity claims a moral certainty, to anyone who is willing to take the evidence and weigh and evaluate it. Christianity claims an external verification through evidence, as well as an internal witness through God.

To those outside the Christian faith, Christianity can be shown to rest on strong evidence and have a high degree of probability for its truth claims. But when a person becomes a Christian, the "assurance" or "certainty" becomes a reality. Christianity from a "morally certain" standpoint becomes as undeniable as one's own existence.

Between the two of us, we have spoken to millions of students, professors, businessmen, and laymen about the evidence for the Bible and Jesus Christ. We have probably not met more than a half dozen people who, after hearing the facts, still claimed an intellectual problem with accepting Christianity as true.

The problem is not a matter of "I can't believe because the facts won't let me" so much as a matter of "No matter what proof, I won't believe." If anyone is truly interested in evaluating the evidence for proof of Christianity's truth, the words of Jesus are applicable: "If any man is willing to do His will, he shall know of the teaching, whether it is of God, or whether I speak from Myself" (John 7:17, NASB).

✚ ADDITIONAL REFERENCE SOURCES

John Warwick Montgomery, "Sensible Christianity," tape series, P.O. Box 500, San Juan Capistrano, Calif. 92693

Colin Chapman, *Christianity on Trial*, Tyndale House Publishers, 1975

Are Christians guilty of circular reasoning?

A charge that is frequently leveled against the Bible is that Christians argue in circles. The charge goes that Christians claim the Bible is the inspired Word of God and, as a proof of this contention, they quote a passage from the Bible that says so.

This type of argumentation is known as begging the question, or circular reasoning. Nothing is proved in this type of argumentation. It is based on assuming something to be true, using that assumption as fact to prove another assumption and using the "proved" assumption to prove your original assumption!

Some Christians (and many non-Christians!) do argue in circles, but about the Bible they certainly don't need to.

Instead of assuming the Bible is the Word of God, we can begin by demonstrating that the Scriptures are basically reliable and trustworthy historical documents. This is confirmed by applying the ordinary test of historical criticism to the Scriptures.

Once it is established that the Bible is a valid historical record, the next point is realizing that Jesus Christ claims to be the unique Son of God and that He bases this claim on His forthcoming resurrection from the dead.

Next, we examine the evidence for the resurrection contained in this historic document and find that the arguments overwhelmingly support the contention that Christ has risen from the dead. If this is true, then He is the unique Son of God as He claimed to be. If He is indeed God, then He speaks with authority on all matters.

Since Jesus considered the Old Testament to be the Word of God (Matthew 15:1–4; 5:17, 18) and promised His disciples, who either wrote or had control over the writing of the New Testament books, that the Holy Spirit would bring all things back to their remembrance (John 14:26), we can insist, with sound and accurate logic, that the Bible is God's word. This is not circular reasoning. It is establishing certain facts and basing conclusions on the sound logical outcome of these facts. The case for Christianity can be established by ordinary means of historical investigation.

✚ ADDITIONAL REFERENCE SOURCES

J. W. Montgomery, *Where is History Going?* Bethany Fellowship

Arlie J. Hoover, *Dear Agnos*, Baker Book House, 1976

Q

Does it really matter what I believe?

A question we hear often is, "Does it really matter what I believe as long as I believe in something?" Or, "As long as your belief helps you, isn't that all that matters?"

The idea behind statements such as these is that there is no absolute truth to believe in, and thus the act of believing is all there is. We all believe in something, as Edgar Sheffield Brightman states, "A thinker cannot divest himself of real convictions, and it is futile to pose as having none" (E.S. Brightman in H.N. Wieman, B.E. Meland (eds.), *American Philosophies of Religion*, New York, Harper & Brothers, 1936).

The idea of finding any truth or meaning to life has escaped modern man. This statement reflects the inability to conceive of something outside of one's self: "There are no rules by means of which we would discover a purpose or a meaning of the universe" (Hans Reichenbach, *The Rise of Scientific Philosophy*, p. 301).

Even though we live in a day in which we all have definite beliefs about things, the climate seems to be the act of belief rather than any real object of belief. "Be not afraid of life. Believe that life is worth living, and your belief will help create the fact," states pragmatist William James.

Unfortunately, this is not the case. Belief will not create fact. Truth is independent of belief. No matter how hard I may try, believing something will not make it true. For example, I may believe with all my heart that I want it to snow tomorrow, but this will not guarantee snow. Or I may believe that my run-down old car is really a new Rolls Royce, but my belief won't change the fact.

Belief is only as good as the object in which we put our trust. Someone may come to me and say, "Hey, let's go for a ride in my new plane!" If I come to find out that his plane hardly runs at all and he does not even have a pilot's license, then my faith, no matter how *much* I have, is not well-founded.

My faith won't create a great pilot out of my friend once we are in the sky! However, if another friend of mine comes along and makes the same offer, but he is a certified pilot with a new plane, then my trust has a much more solid base. So it does matter what I believe, for my believing it does not make it true.

The Bible also emphasizes the fact that it is vital what one believes. Jesus said, "If you do not believe that I am He, you will die in your sins" (John 8:24, MLB). We are also told, "He that believeth on the Son hath everlasting life: and he that believeth not the Son shall not see life; but the wrath of God abideth on him" (John 3:36, KJV).

Thus, the stress of the Scriptures is not so much on the *act* of belief as on the *object* of belief. What is emphasized is not so much the one trusting, but rather the one trusted. Jesus said, "I am the way, the truth, and the life: no man cometh unto the Father, but by Me" (John 14:6, KJV).

People today are believing whatever they wish to believe, but this will lead to their ultimate destruction. The famous classroom story of the philosopher, Georg Hegel, illustrates the type of faith many people display, which is entirely unbiblical. Hegel, as the story goes, was expounding on his philosophy of history with reference to a particular series of events when one of his students objected to Hegel's view and replied, "But, Herr Professor, the facts are otherwise."

"So much worse for the facts," was Hegel's answer.

One of the darkest periods in the history of Israel occurred in the time of the kings. During this time, there was a contest between the Lord God and Baal, a highly regarded cult deity.

An altar of wood was built, with pieces of an oxen laid upon it as a sacrifice. The god who answered by fire and consumed the sacrifice would be acknowledged as the true god in Israel. Baal went first.

If anyone could start a fire from the sky, it was Baal—the great nature god who controlled the weather (e.g., rain, thunderstorms, lightning). The priests of Baal paraded around the altar all morning and until late afternoon, beseeching Baal to respond.

These false priests jumped all over the altar, cut themselves with swords, danced into a frenzy, raved and pleaded all day. Yet nothing happened. No one can say they were not sincere or did not believe.

After they were finished and the altar was rebuilt, the Lord God answered with fire from heaven and consumed the altar and sacrifice. The false prophets of Baal were then slain.

If sincerity and belief saved, then these prophets should have been spared. But they do not. These prophets had their trust in the wrong object. They had never chosen to investigate the truth. God requires man to put his faith in Jesus Christ; nothing less will satisfy either them or Him.

Why does a good God allow evil to exist?

One of the most haunting questions we face concerns the problem of evil. Why is there evil in the world if there is a God? Why isn't He doing something about it? Many assume that the existence of evil disproves the existence of God.

Sometimes the problem of evil is put to the Christian in the form of a complex question, "If God is good, then He must not be powerful enough to deal with all the evil and injustice in the world since it is still going on. If He is powerful enough to stop wrongdoing then He Himself must be an evil God since He's not doing anything about it even though He has the capability. So which is it? Is He a bad God or a God that's not all powerful?" Even the biblical writers complained about pain and evil. "Evils have encompassed me without number" (Psalm 40:12, RSV). "Why is my pain unceasing, my wound incurable, refusing to be healed?" (Jeremiah 15:18, RSV). "The whole creation has been groaning in travail together until now" (Romans 8:22, RSV). Thus we readily admit that evil is a problem and we also admit that if God created the world the way it is today He would not be a God of love but rather an evil God.

However the Scriptures make it plain that God did not create the world in the state in which it is now, but evil came as a result of the selfishness of man. The Bible says that God is a God of love and He desired to create a person and eventually a race that would love Him. But genuine love cannot exist unless freely given through free choice and will, and thus man was given the choice to accept God's love or to reject it. This choice made the possibility of evil become very real. When

Adam and Eve disobeyed God, they did not choose something God created, but, by their choice, they brought evil into the world. God is neither evil nor did He create evil. Man brought evil upon himself by selfishly choosing his own way apart from God's way.

Because of the fall, the world now is abnormal. Things are not in the state that they should be in. Man, as a result of the fall, has been separated from God. Nature is not always kind to man and the animal world can also be his enemy. There is conflict between man and his fellow man. None of these conditions were true before the fall. Any solution that might be given to the problems mankind faces must take into consideration that the world as it stands now is not normal.

Although evil is here and it is real, it is also temporary. Evil will eventually be destroyed. This is the hope that the believer has. There is a new world coming in which there will be no more tears or pain because all things will be made new (Revelation 21:5). Paradise lost will be paradise regained. God will right every wrong and put away evil once for all, in His time.

Christians have a justification for fighting evil, immorality, and corruption. The world was not designed with evil in mind and the believer has a real basis for fighting social ills. He is not following the belief that whatever is, is right. The Christian does not condone wrongdoing by claiming it is God's world, neither does he assume that everything that happens is agreed to by God. God does not desire evil nor does He ever condone it. He hates evil, and the Christian also is not only to despise evil, he is obligated to do something about it. Even though sin is real, it is not something that the believer accepts as the way things ought to be. By identifying with Jesus, the believer has a duty to call things wrong that are wrong and to speak out when evil is overtaking good. The Christian is not fighting against God by fighting social problems. Natural disasters, crime, and mental retardation should not be the accepted order of things, because they were never meant to be and they will not be in God's future kingdom.

However, some people are still bothered that God even allows evil in the first place. They question His wisdom in giving man a choice in the matter. Dorothy Sayers put the problem of evil in the proper perspective: "For whatever reason God chose to make man as he is—limited and suffering and subject to sorrows and death—He had the honesty and the courage to take His own medicine. Whatever game He is playing with His creation, He has kept His own rules and played fair. He can exact nothing from man that He has not exacted from Himself. He has Himself gone through the whole of human experience, from the trivial irritations of family life and the cramping restrictions of hard work and lack of money to the worst horrors of pain and humiliation, defeat, despair and death. When He was a man, He played the man. He was born in poverty and died in disgrace and thought it well worth while" (Dorothy Sayers, *Creed or Chaos?* New York: Harcourt, Brace and Col, 1949, p.4).

The Bible tells us that God's purposes are sometimes beyond our understanding. "'For My thoughts are not your thoughts, neither are your ways My ways,' declares the Lord. 'For as the heavens are higher than the earth, so are My ways higher than your ways, and My thoughts than your thoughts'" (Isaiah 55:8, 9, NASB). Paul, in a similar vein, wrote to the church at Rome, "Oh, the depth of the riches both of the wisdom and knowledge of God! How unsearchable are His judgments and unfathomable His ways" (Romans 11:33, NASB).

Although the Bible informs us how and why evil came about, it does not tell us why God allowed it to happen. However, we do know that God is all-wise and all-knowing and that He has reasons for allowing things to happen that are beyond our comprehension.

✚ ADDITIONAL REFERENCE SOURCES

C. S. Lewis, *The Problem of Pain*, MacMillan, 1950

Norman Geisler, *The Roots of Evil*, Zondervan Probe Ministries, 1978

Alvin Plantinga, *God, Freedom, and Evil*, Eerdmans, 1977

Walter Martin, "Evil and Human Suffering," (tape), Christian Research Institute, Box 500, San Juan Capistrano, Calif. 92693

Don Stewart, "God and Evil", (tape), The Word for Today, P.O. Box 8000, Costa Mesa, Calif. 92626

Q Is the Shroud of Turin the authentic burial cloth of Christ?

A The Shroud of Turin, an ancient linen cloth 14 feet by 4 feet, has been hailed around the world as the genuine burial garment of Jesus. Scores of people have supported its authenticity. Pope Paul VI proclaimed the Shroud to be "the most important relic in the history of Christianity" (*U. S. Catholic*, May 1978, p. 48).

The image on the cloth is purported to be the very image of Jesus Christ and demonstrates tangible proof of Christ's death, burial, and resurrection. Many have called it the world's greatest mystery. The Shroud's proponents claim that the image stands up to twentieth century analysis as being humanly impossible to "fake" or "duplicate."

After quite extensive research, we have come to view the Shroud with great skepticism. It seems that much of the Shroud research has been accomplished in the light of preconceived convictions about the cloth's authenticity.

There are many accurate problems with holding that the Shroud is authentic. Prior to 1350, there is no historical evidence to prove authenticity or even the existence of the Shroud. A. J. Otterbein in *The New Catholic Encyclopedia* observes:

"The incomplete documentation on the Shroud makes some hesitant to accept its authenticity. Such hesitancy is justified if one considers only the historical evidence."

Forgery

About 1900, a letter was found in a collection of documents owned by Ulysse Chevalier. The letter was written in 1389 by the Bishop of Troyes to the Anti-Pope of Avignon, Clement the VII.

The letter explained that an investigation had exposed the artist who had painted the Shroud and he had confessed. Many were disturbed that the cloth was being used for financial gain. The letter further pointed out:

"For many theologians and other wise persons declared that this could not be the real Shroud of our Lord, having the Savior's likeness thus imprinted upon it, since the Holy Gospel made no mention of any such imprint; while, if it had been true, it was quite unlikely that the holy evangelist would have omitted to record it, or that the fact should have remained hidden until the present time."

The letter added that the forger had been exposed and referred to "the truth being attested by the artist who had painted it, to wit, that it was a work of human skill and not miraculously wrought or bestowed."

Its History

Geoffrey de Charney acquired the Shroud sometime before 1357. It was displayed for veneration in 1357 at a collegiate church in Lirey, France, founded by Geoffrey. However, Geoffrey died in 1356 before he had revealed how he had obtained the cloth.

The Shroud was put into storage when an investigation showed it to be a fake. Then, about 1449 Margaret de Charney, Geoffrey's granddaughter, toured with the cloth and charged an admission fee. In 1452, she gave the Shroud to the Duke of Savoy in exchange for two castles.

It was housed in the Sainte Chapelle of Chambery where a fire damaged it on December 3, 1532.

Emmanuel Philibert of Savoy moved the Shroud from France to Turin, Italy in 1578. A photographer by the name of Secondo Pia photographed the cloth's image in 1898. To everyone's surprise it was discovered that the imprint on the cloth was a negative.

Image Creation

The transference of the image to the cloth is an important step in explaining whether or not the cloth is a result of a miracle and is in fact the burial cloth of Jesus. If there was no doubt that the cloth was beyond natural means, we would have a miracle and therefore the cloth of Christ. It is admitted by both sides in this argument that the image is patterned after Christ's crucifixion.

The methods proposed for the transfer of the image to the cloth are (1) vaporography; (2) scorching and radiation; and (3) thermography.

Vaporography is a process by which the mixture of spices, aloes, and oil reacts with the ammonia (urea) in a man's sweat in the form of vapors to form an image on the cloth. The only requirement of physics is that the vapors must travel in straight lines to form the image.

The problem with this theory is that not all chemists believe vapors will travel in exact linear relationships from their points of origin. O'Gorman wrote in 1931 that a possible way for a vapograph to take place would be with the addition of a radioactive substance in the spices or the body of Christ Himself! But this must be recognized as speculation of the highest nature.

Another method that has gained popularity and is dealt with in the "Proceedings" is "scorching," or the process of a body releasing radiation sufficient enough to burn the image onto the cloth. This theory was put to rest by the testimony of two scientists, Wade Patterson and Dave S. Myers of the Lawrence Livermore Laboratory.

They said they didn't see any way that the Shroud images could have been produced naturally by ionizing or high-energy radiation, nuclear or otherwise. X-rays and gamma rays are among the principal ionizing rays, and the images couldn't have been produced by either of them because it takes high-voltage machines to generate X-rays and the only natural sources of gamma rays are radioactive substances like uranium; besides, X-rays and gamma rays don't act on matter in the ways shown on the Shroud.

X-rays and gamma rays, they continued, are among the most penetrating radiations; they would have gone right through the Shroud instead of marking it. A very intense source of ionizing radiation, they admitted, would have been able to affect the cloth, but, given the factors involved—a body, the passage of centuries, and so on—they didn't see how that could have been possible.

Even if by some unlikely chance the body had been made radioactive and was therefore emanating X-rays or gamma rays, the images on the Shroud were still not in accordance with the kinds of images that should have formed under these circumstances. X-rays and gamma rays are more strongly absorbed by the bones, said Patterson, and thus bones, and not skin, would have been the most distinguishable aspects of the images.

Even if a radioactive substance such as uranium—which emits gamma rays and alpha and beta particles, all of which are ionizing radiations—had been smeared on the body, the scientists still didn't think the Shroud images would have appeared; at best there would have been a sillhouette.

If a radioactive substance had been applied in such a way as to emphasize only highlights, they added, they still didn't know of any technique for sensitizing cloth so that it would be able to register high-energy radiation. X-rays were an example of what they meant; film is needed to record the presence of X-rays.

If an atomic blast had gone off over Jerusalem at the time of the burial, there would have been enough high-energy radiation to etch the images on the Shroud, but it would have destroyed the Shroud itself with its intensity. Even if it didn't destroy the Shroud, it would have affected the linen of the Shroud in a quite different way (from *The Shroud*, by Wilcox, pp. 154, 155).

A third method that would allow for an image transfer is a lower form of radiation manifested in the mode of heat. This process is called thermography, and it is used in the detection of breast cancer. Drs. Jackson and Jumper favor this method as the most probable for the image transfer.

"Using computers to analyze data from the photos, they had verified the idea that the image was uniformly lighter and darker in proportion to the distance between the body and the cloth. So uniform, in fact, was the variation . . . that there was no question in their minds that images had been produced by some 'physical process'—apparently other than human artistry—and they tended to favor a 'thermogram,' an image formed by heat" (From *The Shroud*, by Wilcox, p. 175).

However, Dr. Wood of the Neurological Institute of New York relates this process to the Shroud and as a result exposes significant doubt on this process.

Thermography, explained Dr. Ernest Wood, grew out of infrared photography which was developed in World War II; today it is used mainly in the detection of breast cancer. The principle behind it is a simple one: heat emanating from the body is used to make diagnostic pictures, and the pictures are negatives.

But there were significant differences, Dr. Wood pointed out, between thermographic pictures and the "pictures" on the Shroud. For one thing, it took sophisticated machines to magnify body heat to the extent that a picture could be registered: the magnification was on the order of one million times. For another, the thermographic picture was registered on Polaroid film, not cloth (from *The Shroud*, by Wilcox, pp. 171, 172).

The amount of radiated heat magnified on a scale of a million times or more would in all probability destroy the cloth with its intensity.

Those who advocate that low radiation made the image must provide for a refraction of the visible light. They account for this by the supposed layer of morbid sweat on the body acting as a refraction lens to focus the radiation in the necessary linear columnated pattern to produce the image (hence a major reason why the body must be unwashed).

If you remove the sweat, you remove the mechanism for focusing. Dr. Mueller called this whole theory ridiculous, as the body would require hundreds of lenses all over it resembling a fly's eye to focus the radiation. Sweat would just not do it!

It is also important that the visible low-level radiation being discussed form the image at less than two inches from the body. At greater distances, the radiation intensity drops to zero and would not leave an image.

The average for the distance on the Shroud is three centimeters or one-and-a-half inches, which significantly weakens the image-forming properties of radiation, and there are much greater distances on the Shroud to be covered which should form no image if the cause was a radiation scorch.

It is also important to remember that the proponents' mechanism for radiation scorch is all pure speculation; there is no proof. It must be wild guessing at best.

Dr. Marvin Mueller has been with the Los Almos Scientific Laboratory in New Mexico for twenty years, and has done experimental and theoretical research in several different fields of physics. For the past eight years he has worked on the Laser Fusion Energy Project, and is internationally known in this field for his theoretical contributions and antagonistic efforts.

In a letter, Dr. Mueller writes: "Some scientists who are members of the Shroud of Turin Research Project (STURP) have claimed that the experimental results of their study show the Shroud did in fact wrap the crucified body of Jesus Christ.

"Their main reason for asserting the authenticity of the Shroud is based on the claim that the Shroud image would only have been produced by a 'short burst of radiation' emanating from the body and then scorching the image of the body onto the cloth with which it was covered.

"Such an event would of course be miraculous, but that is just what they need to establish authenticity; for no natural process of image formation could lead to the conclusion that the body which produced the image was that of Jesus Christ.

"However, their assertions do not withstand close examination, and seem to be based in large measure on wishful thinking. For one thing, they have *not* demonstrated that the Shroud image is a scorch, although it does possess some scorch-like properties such as color and heat resistance.

"Other substances, which could have been used to form the image of artistic means, also possess these properties and have in fact been found on the image. This fact alone makes any claim of authenticity seem rather foolish.

"Moreover, the STURP has *not* demonstrated that the image was transferred through space from body to cloth by means of radiation or any other agent. While the details are too complicated to be explained here, it can be said that all STURP has done is to establish a correlation between Shroud image density (darkness) and cloth-to-body distances measured using a male volunteer overlaid with a cloth.

"But correlation does not imply causality. For example, in principle at least, the procedure which STURP uses to construct a statue of the 'Man of the Shroud' could also be used to reconstruct a full relief (or statue) from a rubbing image produced by Joe Nickells' method.

"The fact that they have produced a statue from the Shroud image using the method outlined says nearly nothing about the method by which the image was produced. In particular, the rubbing method, being intrinsically variable and adaptable, can produce a wide range of tonal gradations for a given bas-relief; and can thereby vary the 'three-dimensional' characteristics of the image almost at will.

"Hence, the two assertions on which the 'short burst of radiation' hypothesis is based are not defensible. Any claim for authenticity of the Shroud of Turin is so premature as to be ludicrous."

3-D Image

One claim of the Shroud proponents is that the image on the cloth can be reproduced into a 3-D image with an Interpretations Systems YP-8 Image Analyzer. This equipment is supposed to transfer tonal values into a three-dimensional relief or image with very little adjustment.

Drs. Jackson and Jumper observe: "A well-known argument has been that an artist, who must have lived prior to the 14th century, could not have produced a consistent negative image without the capability of checking his work by photographic inversion.

"Similarly, we submit that an artist or forger living then would not have been able to encode three-dimensional information by adjusting the intensity levels of this work to everywhere correspond to actual cloth-body separations.

"To demonstrate this point, we performed an experiment. We obtained photographs of Shroud paintings by two competent artists who had been commissioned to copy the Shroud as exactly as possible.

"Then, we transformed these pictures into relief images to see how well each artist had captured the three dimensionality of the Shroud onto his painting. At the time, both artists were not aware of the three-dimensional property.

"Varying the degree of relief did not help the situation because the abnormalities of these pictures were only altered proportionally, but not eliminated. Since two competent artists who had the Shroud itself to copy were unable to flawlessly produce a three-dimensional image from the Shroud, it would seem remote that some medieval artist could have achieved such an accomplishment with no Shroud available for reference.

"In fact, we consider it a challenge for pre-twentieth century technology to have placed a clear three-dimensional image of a human body onto a cloth either by artistry or any other means available" (from *The 1977 Research Proceedings on the Shroud of Turin*, p. 85).

John German, a colleague of Drs. Jackson and Jumper, points out that the quality of the image is dependent upon how equipment is focused:

"The nature of this relationship revealed an important source of error inherent in the construction of the three-dimensional image of the Shroud. The image on the cloth was formed by a process that resulted in a non-linear relationship between the image intensity and the cloth-body distance.

"The image analyzer system, however, creates a three-dimensional image for which the relief (analogous to cloth-body distance) varies linearly with the intensity. The practical result of this linear relationship is that the image is distorted. If the gain (amount of relief) is reduced to produce an image with a realistic nose and forehead, the fainter portions of the image corresponding to large cloth-body distances have little or no relief.

"On the other hand, if the gain is increased to bring out these fainter portions of the image, the nose and forehead grow way out of proportion" (from *Proceedings*, p. 235).

The question here is with the lenses that are used to correct tonal distortions and a machine that relies heavily on simulation: Is the 3-D image of the Shroud so perfect as to be considered miraculous?

It must also be considered that in order to get the necessary image, a human model approximating the Shroud's image is needed to correlate the distance of cloth to body interfaces.

After that, the cloth on the model must be smoothed (resulting in distortion) and then camera images imposed upon the cloth distance correlations. The question here is: how can you know you have reproduced a 3-D image of the Shroud or just the Shroud's image on an actual man?

Dr. Marvin Mueller, Ph.D. in physics of the Los Alamos Lab, states:

"The relative image darkness is determined by optically scanning a photograph of the Shroud image. Next, a correlation plot of image darkness vs. cloth-body distance is made. To maximize the correlation numerous adjustments are made in the detailed drape shape of the cloth.

"The final adjusted correlation is fairly good, and a smoothly declining function approximating an exponential is extracted. However, except for measurement errors and except for the smoothing involved in extracting the function from scattered data, one winds up with just a 3-D relief of the human model chosen for the experiment!

"The irony is that the smoothing process itself produces distortion of the relief, but it also affords the possibility that some of the characteristics of the Shroud image can now be superimposed on the relief of the human model chosen for the experiment!

"Thus, the resultant 'statue' is some blend of the characteristics of the human model and the Shroud image—not, as has been asserted, a statue of the Man of the Shroud.

"What STURP has done is to demonstrate it can obtain a fairly good correlation between the image darkness on the Shroud and the corresponding cloth-body distance obtained when a particular male body of the proper size is overlaid with a particular cloth draped in a certain way. But, because correlation is not causality, that is all STURP has done" (from *The Los Alamos Monitor*, December 16, 1979, p. B–6).

Blood Stains

Alleged blood stains on two small particles and twelve threads of the Shroud were analyzed for authenticity. Prior to recent testing done on the Shroud, it was determined by the scientists that no conclusive evidence existed for the stains on the cloth being human blood (Thomas Humber, *The Sacred Shroud*, p. 178). Recent tests conducted in 1978 have led protagonists to believe that "the blood stained areas had spectral-characteristics of human hemoglobin" (S. F. Pellicori, "Spectral Properties of the Shroud of Turin," *Applied Optics*, 15 June 1980, Vol. 19, No. 12, pp. 1913–1920). However, the issue still remains that a forger with a proper method would logically use human blood to create the most realistic image possible. The presence of blood or hemoglobin on the Shroud is not valid evidence to warrant claims of authenticity.

Duplication

The Shroud proponents set forth various pieces of evidence to support their claims of authenticity. Such pieces of evidence were (1) no brush mark; (2) no image penetration of the fibers (it is purely a surface phenomenon); (3) presence of a powder alleged to be aloes; (4) the "pollen fossils" found on the cloth alleged to be from the time of Christ.

Most of the above is answered by a bas-relief image created by Joe Nickell. A picture of the image is found in the November–December 1978 issue of *The Humanist* and in the November 1979 issue of *Popular Photography*.

Nickell employed a technique using only fourteenth century material and methods to recreate or duplicate a negative imagery as found on the Shroud. This technique produces a negative.

He did not paint his image, but used a bas-relief and applied a wet cloth to it, and when it had dried he used a dauber to rub on powdered "pigment." Nickell used a mixture of myrrh and aloes. It did not leave brush marks.

Nickell writes: "My rubbings, even on close inspection, appear to have been created without 'pigment.' I used a mixture of the burial spices—myrrh and aloes—which duplicates the 'scorch-like' color and numerous characteristics.

"It is interesting to note that (according to *Encyclopedia Americana*, 1978) aloes actually have 'served as a dye or pigment.'

"A major point is that this 'pigment' does not penetrate the fibers, remaining (as is said of the coloration on the Shroud) a purely 'surface phenomenon'—shown by cross-sectioning and microscopic examination . . .

"Two members of the secret (and later exposed) official Shroud commission, appointed in 1969 to examine the cloth, suggested the imagery was the result of some *artistic* printing technique employing a model or molds. That is a pretty accurate description of the technique I found to be successful.

"Shroud enthusiasts maintain they have found 'no evidence of pigment' on the cloth, although there is reportedly evidence of a 'powder' said to be aloes. They point out that there are no brush strokes; that, around the burn holes (from a chapel fire in 1532), there is no darkening of imprinted areas; and that the imagery has 'no directionality' (as from brush or finger application). These, however, are all characteristics of my technique!

"The report did mention the discovery of various yellow-red to orange 'crystals' (or 'granules') and certain 'globules' which tally with the appearance of myrrh and aloes. These spices (available to the forger at the twice-a-year Champagne Fair or at his local apothecary's) probably contained the 'pollen fossils' from the Middle East that are alleged to be on the cloth" ("The Shroud," *Christian Life*, February 1980, vol. 4, no. 10).

A photographer's negative showed a positive image of "lifelike" quality. Dr. Mueller says of Nickells' image:

"Joe Nickell describes his rubbing method of producing Shroud-like negative images from bas-reliefs. Qualitatively, at least, the resemblance is striking and extends even to the microscopic depth of color penetration of the threads.

"The rubbing technique, even with a given bas-relief, can be varied easily by changing dauber size, pressure and the way the cloth is wet-moulded to produce images of greatly diverse character. Thus, the 3-D characteristics of rubbings can be varied almost at will" ("Shroud: Real McCoy or Hoax?" *Los Alamos Monitor*, December 16, 1979).

Christ's Graveclothes

Probably the most damaging evidence against the authenticity of the Shroud is the disharmony of the Shroud burial procedure with the New Testament accounts of Christ's burial.

"In ancient times the hair was cut (T. B., Moed. Kat., 8b), but it is now only washed, and nine measures of cold water are subsequently poured over the corpse (during which, in some places, the dead is settled in an upright position), and this constitutes the actual religious purification . . .

"The corpse is, of course, thoroughly dried, care being taken not to leave it uncovered the while. Women have to undergo the same process of purification at the hands of their own sex. In Acts 9:37 we have an instance of a woman being washed before burial in New Testament times.

"It was formerly the custom also the anoint the corpse, after cleansing, with various kinds of aromatic spices. . . . It will be remembered that when Mary was reproached with an unnecessary waste of ointment, Jesus exclaimed, 'Suffer her to keep it against the day of my burial' (John 12:7). And we find it recorded that a mixture of myrrh and aloes, about 100 lbs. weight, was subsequently brought for the body of Jesus (*Ibid* 9:39).

"After the rite of purification has been carried out in the customary manner, the corpse is clothed in grave-vestments (*Mish. Sanhed.* 6.5) . . . They are identical with the *sindon* of the New Testament (cf. Matthew 27:59, etc.) being made of white linen without the slightest ornament, and must be stainless.

"They are usually the work of women, and are simply pieced together, no knots being permitted, according to some, in token that the mind of the dead is disentangled of the cares of this life, but in the opinion of others, as representing the expression of a wish that the bones of the dead may be speedily dissolved into their primitive dust (*Rokeach*, 316). No corpse, male or female, must be clothed in less than three garments" (from *The Jewish Quarterly Review*, vol. 7, 1895, pp. 260, 261).

There are several problems that arise when Shroud proponents study the New Testament. The first is that there is a conflict with the burial cloth. It is clear in the Jewish burial customs and in the New Testament that there were several pieces of cloth involved in Christ's burial, not one 14-feet-by-4-feet piece of material such as the Shroud.

John 20:5–7 clearly indicates there was a separate piece wrapped about Christ's head. It was found by itself apart from the body wrappings. However, the cloth of Turin depicts a fact on the sheet as well as the rest of the body.

Not only does the text indicate several pieces of cloth used for Christ's body, but also that they were "strips," "wrappings," or "linen bandages" such as used with mummies.

Even more significant than the words used to describe Christ's burial with strips of linen are *Kalutto* (I Kings 19:13) and *Periballo* (Genesis 38:14) which are words used in the Septuagint specifically for garments such as the Shroud but not found in the New Testament texts. Their absence is quite significant.

Second, the burial account in the Gospel of John (19:40) uses a plural form: *wrappings*. In fact, all of the Gospel accounts are in agreement that the body of Christ was "wrapped" or "folded."

"And Joseph took the body and wrapped it in a clean linen cloth" (Matthew 27:59, NASB).

"And Joseph bought a linen sheet, took Him down, wrapped Him in the linen cloth" (Mark 15:46, NASB).

"And he took it down and wrapped it in a linen cloth" (Luke 23:53, NASB).

"And so they took the body of Jesus, and bound it in linen wrappings with the spices, as is the burial custom of the Jews" (John 19:40, NASB).

The verb *Entulisso*, used by Matthew and Luke, means to wrap (up), to fold. Mark uses *Eneileo*, which connotes to wrap up, to confine. John, who was an eyewitness, is very clear that the body of Christ was wrapped. The verb *Deo* means "to bind" or "tie" with the result of imprisonment.

So in light of the textual evidence, the conclusion is well founded by word choice and placement that, as John most explicitly described, Jesus was *bound* with linen strips and not wrapped in a cloth. The words regarding the cloth clearly indicate it. The verbs used warrant it, and the specific choice of words makes it inescapable.

A third problem with the cloth of Turin is that the Shroud proponents admit that its authenticity is dependent upon the body not being washed. This is important for several reasons: (1) the alleged appearance of dried blood on the body that was not washed, and (2) the need for morbid sweat to act as a refraction lens to focus the radiation to record the image.

Ian Wilson expresses the view that Christ's body was not washed. He writes:

"Some have argued that washing was a prescribed ritual that would have been permissible to carry out irrespective of the sabbath. Some eminent New Testament scholars do not share such a view. Even among the best exegetes there seems little major objection to the concept that there simply was on time for Jesus' body to be washed before the sabbath, particularly in view of the various Jewish requirements relating to this rite.

"When, as events proved, it was also impossible to carry out this rite after the sabbath, one can understand a certain reluctance on the part of the Gospel writers to admit this directly. *Only on the view that Jesus was not washed can the authenticity of the Turin Shroud be upheld*" (from *The Shroud of Turin,* by Ian Wilson, p. 56).

The above conclusions are erroneous at best. The idea of there not being time to wash the body clean with water because of the approaching sabbath is equally weak because the Scripture says they still had time to anoint the body with over a hundred pounds of spices. This is also made clear in the fact that a body could indeed be washed and anointed on the sabbath:

"The corpse may, however, be washed and anointed on the sabbath, provided the limbs be not strained out of joint; the pillow may be moved from under the head, and the body may be laid on sand that it keep the longer from putrefaction; the jaws may also be tied, not to force them closer, but to prevent them dropping lower (*Mish. Shabb.* 33:5, from *The Jewish Quarterly Review*, 1895, vol. 7, p. 118).

John would not and could not have said that the Jewish method of burial had been followed if it hadn't been washed.

The Spices

A fourth problem with harmonizing the Shroud with the New Testament burial accounts is the spices. The body would have had to have been washed. Ian Wilson observes:

"St. John tells us that Nicodemus, assisting Joseph of Arimathea, brought a mixture of myrrh and aloes weighing about a hundred pounds. He also tells us that these were wrapped with the body in the burial linen (John 19:39, 40).

"Had such spices been used for anointing, it would have been requisite in Jewish ritual and indeed in that of any other culture to wash the body first.

"As it is quite evident from the Shroud that the body was not washed, and as the weight of spices described would be vastly excessive even for the most lavish anointing, the most likely explanation would seem to be that they were dry blocks of aromatics packed around the body as antiputrefacients" (from *The Shroud of Turin*, by Wilson, pp. 56, 57).

Also, if spices were applied to the body, as emphatically stated in the Gospels, the image could not have been transferred to the cloth by radiation as Shroud proponents advocate.

Other Shrouds

Many people are not cognizant of the fact that after the Crusades many different Shrouds circulated throughout medieval Europe at the same time as the cloth of Turin. It is estimated there are more than forty "true Shrouds" that were circulated. Many are still being displayed today.

Coins

Reports are being circulated of a coin over the right eye that dates back to the years of A.D. 29–32. The Reverend Francis L. Philas, Professor of Theology at Loyola University in Chicago, reports that four Greek letters, UCAI, on the coin are part of the inscription "of Tiberius Caesar."

It is the authors' understanding that the quite unintelligible letters read, UKAI, and that the coin striker would have had to be either drunk or ignorant to strike it that way. The coin theory raises a lot of questions concerning the Shroud. The theory to explain the image transfer to the cloth required that the body had not been washed because the dried sweat was necessary to magnify the rays. Also, the various image transfer theories indicate that the body had not been prepared for burial and thus not washed. It is hard to imagine that a body that had not been washed or prepared for burial would have coins put over the eyes (in this case, over the right eye).

No New Testament Witnesses

It is totally unthinkable that the apostles and Christians of the first years of Christianity would not mention a cloth that had an image scorched on it of the crucified and resurrected Christ. In the face of death they proclaimed Jesus Christ alive. They constantly gave personal testimony of Christ's resurrection appearances in the most adverse situations. Is it conceivable that no one, especially the New Testament writers and church fathers, would ever mention the Shroud in relationship to Christ and His resurrection?

Conclusion

The evidence so far in no way supports the Shroud's authenticity as the burial cloth of Christ.

Don't Genesis 1 and 2 contain contradictory accounts of creation?

Throughout the history of the Church, various portions of the Holy Scriptures have been interpreted, analyzed, questioned, dissected, and attacked—and sometimes dismissed—both by theologians and others.

Whenever there is a passage of Scripture that is difficult to explain or understand at first reading, or that seems to contradict some "scientific fact" or in some other way poses an apparent difficulty to the occidental, modern intellect, somebody, somewhere erects a theory to try to resolve the seeming difficulty.

Just such a situation exists with regard to chapters 1 and 2 of the Book of Genesis, which are alleged by many commentators to be two contradictory accounts of creation. 40/

The Radical Critics' Case

According to their theory, the author of the second account (Genesis 2:4–25) had no prior knowledge of the first account in Genesis 1:1–2:4 and when they are joined together they contain hopeless contradictions.

James sums up the position of the critical school quite strongly:

"When it is realised that there are two distinct creation stories in Genesis belonging to two different periods and derived from two different sources, inconsistency becomes intell-

EXPLANATION OF FOOTNOTES: After each quote there will be two sets of numbers divided by a diagonal (example 47/21–23). The number to the left of the diagonal is the reference to the source in the bibliography at the end of this article. The number on the right refers to the page or pages where the quote is located in the reference source.

igible. That it exists at all, however, is sufficient to discredit a theory of divine inspiration that is obviously out of accord with the facts." (16/31)

The critics themselves differ on the nature of the evidence. The relative importance of these differences are summarized by Kitchen, "Only two lines of evidence have been urged in favor of a double narrative: a differing style and theological conception in Genesis 1 and 2, and a supposedly different order of creation in each narrative." (20/118) A sampling of some of the critics' statements will show this to be the major portion of their case.

Rowley, in his discussion of the contradiction between the two chapters, stated:

"The first two chapters of the Bible contain two irreconcilable accounts of the Creation. According to the first account, a man and woman were together as the crown and climax of creation, after the birds and animals, whereas according to the second account the creation of man preceded the creation of the animals and birds while the creation of woman followed their creation." (31/18)

Rowley thus sees a disagreement as to the sequence of creation, a difference in the usage of the divine names, a different conception of God, and a difference in style.

Driver, who wrote just about the last detailed account of the differences, has this to say:

"Chapter 2:4b differs then firstly from chapter 1 in style and form. The style of chapter 1 is stereotyped, measured, and precise; that of 2:4bff is diversified and picturesque; there are no recurring formulae, such as are so marked in chapter 1; the expressions characteristic of chapter 1 are absent here (e.g., to create); and where common ground is touched (as in the account of the formation of man), the narrative is told very differently, and without even any allusion to the representation of chapter 1 (e.g., to the 'image of God').

"Chapter 1 displays, moreover, clear marks of study and deliberate systematization: 2:4bff is fresh, spontaneous, and, at least in a relative sense, primitive.... The present narrative differs secondly from chapter 1 in representation. Both the details and the order of events of creation (insofar as they are mentioned in it, for the narrator deals briefly with everything except what relates directly to man) differ from the statements of chapter 1.

"The earth, instead of emerging from the waters (as in 1:9) is represented as being at first dry (2:5), too dry in fact to support vegetation: the first step in the process of filling it with living forms is the creation of man (2:7), then follows that of beasts and birds (v. 19), and lastly that of woman (v. 21ff); obviously a different order from that of chapter 1." (7/35)

Theodor Gaster, writing from more recent times, noted also, "Attentive readers of the Bible can hardly fail to remark a striking discrepancy between the two accounts of creation of man recorded in the first and second chapters of Genesis." (12/8)

Though the conclusions the critics draw may be disagreed with, it is impossible to deny the following statement from James:

"A comparison between the two creation stories is full of interest, largely because of the striking differences between them, which though more apparent in the Hebrew, may still be recognized in the English translation." (16/37–38)

The harmonists and critics both agree that the two accounts contain differences. The critics assume that the differences came as a result of a mechanical amalgamation by a later editor of two passages from two different documents.

The harmonists contend that the differences are based on differing subject matter and point of view, as Cassuto notes:

"It is manifest that the two sections differ considerably in character. About this there can be no doubt. The divergence is obvious if we approach the text without bias.

"In the first section, we are vouchsafed a sublime vision of the totality of creation, portrayed with great synthetic power, which unifies into a clear and comprehensible order all the endlessly changing categories of existence; we perceive there, enthroned on high, the idea that rises above the accidental, the temporal and the finite, and depicts for us with complete simplicity of expression the vast expanses of the universe to their utmost limits.

"God reveals Himself . . . as a transcendental Being dwelling in His supernal abode without direct contact with creatures.

"On the other hand, the second section contains a graphic and dramatic narrative that captivates the heart with its details, imbued as they are with the magic hues of the oriental imagination, and seeks to inculcate religious and ethical teachings under the guise of actual happenings, addressing itself more to the feelings than to the intellect of the reader.

"YHWH appears there, as we have already noted, in direct touch with His creature man and with the other created beings of His world. The difference, therefore, is profound from several aspects, and only one who closed his eyes to the obvious could deny it." (6/70–71)

Methodology

The arguments and evidence purporting to show contradiction will be discussed first. The case for harmony and the answers to the critics' contentions will be set forth second.

The relative merits and defects of the opposing views will be examined for logical proof, internal consistency, common sense, harmony with knowledge of Hebrew grammar, and ancient literary styles and usages.

In other words, does harmony of chapters 1 and 2—or contradiction—best resolve the issue of apparent differences in the two chapters, and leave the reader with a firm foundation upon which to trust any of the Scriptures? That shall be the test.

General Differences

There can be no denying that the two chapters differ generally, and on the surface, at least, appear to contradict each other in specific detail. The first general difference the critics note is the different usage in divine names.

It is a fact that chapter 1 uses Elohim exclusively, while chapter 2 uses Jehovah-Elohim. (This, along with a discussion of Astruc's reading of Exodus 6:3, will be dealt with in greater detail when discussing the merits and defects of the critics' case.)

The second major difference the critics point out is the different conception of God. The first account sees God as majestic and dignified, aloof from creation, while the second views God as having human-like traits, such as walking, speaking, and acting like a man. The latter account, therefore, is characterized by anthropomorphisms.

The third general difference noted, which is hard to completely distinguish from the two, is actually a compound of different vocabulary, style, and grammar. Elohim, in the first account, is the name of the universal God. He is dignified, aloof. The style of the first account is measured and precise. The vocabulary is distinctive; Elohim creates calls into being, rests, ceases to make.

In the second account, Jehovah, a personal God, the nationalistic God, is in direct touch with His creation. He forms, breathes, plants, makes. The style is more personal, story-telling, with its own vocabulary.

Specific Differences

In addition to the general differences, the critics note specific differences in detail. The first account has creation stemming from primeval waters:

"And the earth was without form, and void; and darkness was upon the face of the deep. And the Spirit of God moved upon the face of the waters" (Genesis 1:2, KJV).

"And God said, Let the waters under the heaven be gathered together unto one place, and let the dry land appear" (Genesis 1:9, KJV).

The second account has creation stemming from arid ground:

"For the Lord God had not caused it to rain upon the earth" (Genesis 2:5, KJV).

The second and third major differences in detail are the creation of man and the sequence of creation. In the first chapter, man and woman are created simultaneously, after vegetation and animals.

"And God said, Let the earth bring forth grass, the herb yielding seed, and the fruit tree yielding fruit after his kind, whose seed is in itself, upon the earth: and it was so" (Genesis 1:11, KJV).

"And God created great whales, and every living creature that moveth, which the waters brought forth abundantly, after their kind, and every winged fowl after his kind: and God saw that it was good" (Genesis 1:21, KJV).

"And God said, Let the earth bring forth the living creature after his kind, cattle, and creeping thing, and beast of the earth after his kind: and it was so" (Genesis 1:24, KJV).

"So God created man in his own image . . . male and female created he them" (Genesis 1:27, KJV).

In the second chapter, man is created first, then later, after creating vegetation and animals, God forms woman out of man's rib:

"And the Lord God formed man of the dust of the ground, and breathed into his nostrils the breath of life; and man became a living soul" (Genesis 2:7, KJV).

"And the Lord God planted a garden eastward in Eden; and there he put the man whom he had formed" (Genesis 2:8, KJV).

"And out of the ground made the Lord God to grow every tree that is pleasant to the sight, and good for food . . ." (Genesis 2:9, KJV).

"And out of the ground the Lord God formed every beast of the field, and every fowl of the air; and brought them unto Adam . . ." (Genesis 2:19, KJV).

And the Lord God caused a deep sleep to fall upon Adam, and he slept: and he took one of his ribs, and closed up the flesh instead thereof" (Genesis 2:21, KJV).

Driver sums up the critic's attitude by stating, ". . . that the narrator is a different one is so evident as not to need detailed proof." (7/35)

Unity of Plan

As Allis aptly notes, "The word 'generations (toledoth)' occurs in headings 11 times in Genesis (usually in the form: 'these are the generations of'). Consequently, we might expect this word to figure prominently in any analysis of the book." (1/49)

The critics generally recognize this unity; e.g., Driver, quoted earlier. Most of them attribute this unifying phrase, "These are the generations of," to the work of a final redactor, or Priestly (P) writer. Allis elaborates on this:

"But, of course, if similarity of identity of languages proves identity of source, all of these headings should belong to the same document. This had been asserted by Ilgen in 1798, when he divided 2:4 into two parts, treated the first part as the misplaced original heading of the first Elohistic Section, and assigned all the other headings to the same Elohist.

"This drastic but consistent proposal was revived by Noeldeke in 1869 and soon became the generally accepted view of the critics; and they have been asserting ever since with growing positiveness that the 'framework' of Genesis, as determined by these headings, belongs to P, the latest of the sources of Genesis." (1/49–50)

Most of the critics also agree that the phrase is common as a title, but they make an exception of the phrase in chapter 2:4. Von Rad expresses the common assumption of the critics on this usage:

"The statement in chapter 2:4a is difficult. The formula is common in Genesis as a title. . . . Here, however, the passage cannot be a title, for the formula is exclusively Priestly. Another difficulty arises from the use of the word *toledot* in this verse, for the word means 'family tree,' 'genealogy,' literally 'generations.'

"We assume that the formula, which represents a kind of chapter division in the Priestly document, was subsequently added to the chapter on creation because of the need for system. It then was used in this story with the exaggerated meaning, 'story of origin.' Since, however, the beginning of the chapter was canonically fixed, the interpolator had to be satisfied with adding the statement as a concluding word." (29/61)

Though not all critics would agree with everything von Rad said above, in general they all, while recognizing the intended unity, assume this unity was superimposed upon various documents from different sources, leaving contradictions and inconsistencies in the narratives, to embody all the various legends and traditions.

Mythological Derivation

To the internal differences noted above, the critics add the contention that the creation narratives were derived from mythological sources. With an attitude that brooks no disagreement, James states:

"Originally the creation narratives were genuine myths, and there is no escape from the conclusion that they contain a large foreign element. The discovery of the Babylonian Creation stories has put this beyond all reasonable doubt." (16/27–28)

The critical school contends that the beginnings of the human race reach much further back than any written recollections we might possess. There was such a time span between the events and the recording of them that it is not feasible to expect the information to be trustworthy.

They contend that there is not any sufficient reason to suppose that the Hebrews had more trustworthy information concerning the life and condition of the first humans than other nations of the ancient world.

In their point of view, the Hebrew writers offer a picture of primitive times derived from the folklore of other nations. Therefore, it is hardly credible to press for historical details since we are not dealing with recorded history. (7/53)

James closes the case for contradiction with a note of finality when he writes:

"Any artificial attempt to reconcile these marked differences of style, outlook and subject-matter is bound to fail. The recognition that they belong to different periods, the second story being obviously the older and looking back to a still earlier time, is a sufficient and natural explanation of their inconsistency." (16/38)

The traditional position of the Church has been challenged and summarily dismissed.

The Harmonists: Case and Answers

The critics dismissed the traditional teaching with regard to the creation narratives, and, it must be admitted, in some cases rightly scorned the harmonists' attempts to reconcile the narrative to the scientific knowledge of the times.

Many of the harmonists early in this debate seemed intimidated by scientific claims and the overpowering scholarship exhibited by the critics, and were, to reiterate James' words quoted earlier, "driven to the most desperate expedients" to try to answer the critics.

As Taylor Lewis, in his note to Lange's commentary, gently observes, "The attempt, however, of Lange, and of others cited, to reconcile the seeming difficulties can hardly be regarded as giving full satisfaction." (22/201)

Later in his note, he further comments on the attempts to harmonize (in reference to the preparatory recapitulation), "We admit the justness and beauty of the thoughts, but find it difficult to be satisfied with the exposition." (22/201)

To be totally fair to the critics, harmonists had rather ignored a few of the apparent difficulties. But even though the critics feel that the issue is now beyond dispute, in the words of Kidner, "It therefore seems worth pointing out that much of it falls very far short of proof." (19/18)

In the opinion of the harmonists, the critics have misunderstood the nature and the purpose of the account. As Harrison matter-of-factly states:

"It is a mistake to assume that the two Genesis narratives are duplicates, for they actually complement one another. The first outlined the broad process of creation and showed how all things emerged from the creative power of God, while the second paid greater attention to the creation of man and set him with his mate in a specific geographical location." (33/1022)

The material dealing with the creation in the first two chapters of Genesis should be treated as a unit for a correct understanding of the creation and its theological teachings. The second account is complementary to the first, dealing more fully with the creation of our first ancestors, while the initial account gives a description of the world which was being fashioned for Adam and Eve to occupy.

Looking at the problem of differences between the two accounts, the harmonists see complementarity instead of contradiction. Kitchen remarks:

"The strictly complementary nature of the two accounts' is plain enough: Genesis 1 mentions the creation of man as the last of a series, and without any details, whereas in Genesis 2 man is the center of interest and more specific details are given about him and his setting.

"There is not incompatible duplication here at all. Failure to recognize the complementary nature of the subject-distinction between a skeleton outline of all creation on the one hand, and the concentration in detail on man and his immediate environment on the other, borders on obscurantism." (20/116–117)

There is also unmistakable evidence of a close connection between the two chapters that becomes apparent when the problem of evil is considered. How is it possible for the good and beneficent God to have created a world filled with various sorts of evils?

The solution to this question is treating the two sections as one. The former account reveals that the world was initially created very good by the hand of the creator (Genesis 1:31).

The latter account relates how man's transgressions are the cause of all kinds of evil (Genesis 3:6–19). When the two chapters are considered as a continuous whole, the answer is clear, but once the narratives are separated only half of the answer is learned. (6/78)

The lack of cosmology in the alleged second account weakens the argument for contradiction. The latter account, supposedly coming from the hand of J in the ninth century, does not purport to be an account of the creation of the world. It only deals with Adam's creation and the environment in which he was placed.

Gleason Archer observes, "The obvious fact should be noted that no genuine creation account would omit mention of the creation of the sun, moon, stars, earth and seas, as Genesis 2 does." (4/119)

In addition, there is a tacit admission on the part of two of the leading proponents of this theory that the two chapters are not necessarily contradictory.

From Dillman, there is the confession that the second story (chapter 2:4ff) *at least in its present condition* (emphasis added) contains only fragments of a history of creation, but in the main contains something entirely different.

Driver, too, recognizes this fact somewhat grudgingly when he writes:

"The separation between the creation of man and woman, if it stood alone, might indeed be reasonably explained by the supposition that 2:4bff was intended simply as a more detailed account, by the same hand, of what is described summarily in 1:26–39." (7/p35N)

The critics, aware of this difficulty in their arguments, seek to resolve it by invoking a redactor. As Dillman states:

"One would expect that in what follows, either before or after vs. 7, mention would be made of the production of the vegetable world, and completing the formation of the world itself.

"But there is nothing of the sort. There can hardly have been such a gap originally; it rather appears that something has been omitted by R, either because it seemed a needless repetition after chapter 1, or disagreed with chapter 1." (14/23)

James, with even more assurance, alleges, "It may be safely assumed that after having been edited and re-edited, perhaps not once but many times, its present form differs considerably from the original." (16/37)

However, this line of argument makes the critics' case highly suspect. The first chapter places the stress upon divine complacency. This emphasis prepares the way for the fall of man as related in chapter 3.

Chapter 1, therefore, should be regarded as introductory and the basis for the correct understanding of chapter 2. The second chapter assumes the creation of heaven and earth, sun, moon, and stars. Chapter 2, in reality, cannot be understood without chapter 1. (38/55)

Upon close examination, the internal evidence is seen to be in accord with ancient Near Eastern literary practice.

"(The) technique of recapitulation was widely practiced in ancient Semitic literature. The author would first introduce his account with short statement summarizing the whole transaction, and then he would follow it up with a more detailed and circumstantial account when dealing with matters of special importance.

"To the author of Genesis 1, 2 the human race was obviously the crowning or climactic product of creation, and it was only to be expected that he would devote a more extensive treatment to Adam after he had placed him in his historical setting (the sixth creative day)." (4/118)

The two stories of creation are typical of ancient scribble practices, but they are not duplicates, as many of the critical scholars have imagined. In actual fact, they are not even strict repetitions of one another.

The first presents a general description of the creative situation as a whole, while the second account discusses one specific aspect of it, namely man in his physical environment, and then relates it to some particular geographical consideration. (15/554–555)

Developing this thought further, Young writes that "to prepare the way for the account of the fall, chapter 2 gives certain added details about man's original condition, which would have been incongruous and out of place in the grand, declarative march of chapter 1." (38/55)

Allis agrees with this analysis:

"We often find that in describing an event, the biblical writer first makes a brief and comprehensive statement and then follows it with more or less elaborate details. . . . The account given here of the creation of man, generic man, male and female, is followed and expanded in chapter 2 by an account of the creation of Adam (2:7) and of Eve (21–25) which leads up to the account of the fall." (2/82)

The simplest explanation is almost always the best, and what would seem to be the best explanation of the differences in the two chapters is the simplest.

As Taylor Lewis clearly explains, "The internal evidence (shows) that this second account recognizes the first and is grounded upon it, thereby disproving the probability of a contrariety either intended or unseen."

He goes on to state the explanation which he feels "is the one that would most obviously commend itself to the ordinary reader who believed in the absolute truthfulness of the account, and knew nothing of any documentary theory." (22/201)

According to the harmonists, the two narratives are a continuation of the same story. The second account is by the same author as the first, or by one in complete harmony with him.

The latter account refers to all that had been previously stated as the foundation of what is now to be more particularly added concerning man, which may be called the special subject of the second part. (22/201)

The initial account of creation is cosmic and comprehensive. It begins with matter that is formless and ends with man, created in the image of the infinite-personal God. Man is generic, male and female, and is commanded by the creator to be fruitful and multiply, and have dominion over all of the creatures. It is a summary account of divine fiats.

The second account is an expansion of the concluding verses of the first account. It is a "close-up." It does not speak of mankind in general, but the forming of a single pair. The man is fashioned from the dust of the ground, while the first woman is taken from the rib of man. The union of that pair, which is the basis of the commandment to be fruitful and multiply, concludes the first account.

The latter account provides the details which the former narrative omitted. This takes us to the story of the temptation and the fall of this first set of humans who were to be the parents of all mankind. The second account, thus, expands the first by filling in important details that had been omitted. (2/119)

General Differences

In answer to the first general difference the critics note, that of the usage in divine names, the harmonists examine the purpose this has:

"Elohim is plainly the appropriate name for God throughout this section, which regards the Most High as working in nature and in the world at large. True, the creative act may be ascribed to Jehovah (Exodus 20:11), when the thought to be conveyed is that Israel's God, who brought him out of the land of Egypt, was the creator of the world; but when the announcement to be made simply is that the world had a divine creator, Elohim is the proper term, and is hence constantly used in the account of the creation." (14/6)

The name of God is, in the first section, invariably Elohim, while in the second account it is almost as constantly Yahweh-Elohim. This combination would seem to imply that Yahweh is the Elohim who created the world and that both words designate the same being.

Although each designation expresses different attributes of His nature, He is one, and the only maker of the universe. Therefore, the compound term Yahweh-Elohim does not indicate anything opposed to the spirit of the first chapter, but to the contrary it strengthens and confirms it.

This would remove any possible misconception that not Yahweh, as the God of Israel (Exodus 6:3) but, as the universal Lord, Elohim, has created the world. The latter account, by using the name Yahweh, advances a very important step towards the theocratical character of the Pentateuch, and when combining it with the name Elohim reminds us that He is the all-powerful creator. (17/72)

Often liberal scholars will point out the fact that the compound Yahweh-Elohim is nowhere else repeated in Scripture, thus betraying diverse authorship. However, this can be explained by the proper understanding of the purpose of the narratives.

In the first account, the mere external act of the creation of man was narrated, thus it was proper to designate God as the all-powerful being, the God of gods, or Elohim.

In the following section, an internal change takes place in the heart of man by the entrance of sin into the world. Sin now replaces innocence, and misery takes the place of happiness. Therefore, it becomes desirable to introduce God by a name which implies holiness, thus Yahweh-Elohim was employed.

That this idea was in the mind of the writer is evident by the striking fact that in the entire conversation with the serpent, not Yahweh-Elohim, but simply Elohim, is used (Genesis 3:1–5).

It would have been profane to put the divine name into the mouth of the tempter. Thus, with the identity of Elohim and Yahweh having once been impressed, it was not necessary to repeat this later, except on specific occasions. Thus the context determines the proper usage of the name of God. (17/72)

As to the issue of different conceptions of God, Kitchen points out that "the supposed contrast of a transcendent God in Genesis 1 with naive anthropomorphisms in Genesis 2 is vastly overdrawn and, frankly, illusory." (20/118)

Leupold concurs and states, "It should, however, be borne in mind that chapter 1 . . . offered certain very prominent anthropomorphisms, which may very well be classed as arguing a conception of God no different from that of the next two chapters." (23/107)

In conclusion, Young provides details of the anthropomorphisms of chapter 1:

"In chapter 2 an anthropomorphic conception of God is said to appear. God fashions, breathes, plants, places, takes, sets, brings, closes up, builds, walks, etc. But this objection is superficial. An anthropomorphic conception of God also appears in chapter 1.

"Indeed, it is impossible for the finite mind to speak of God without using anthropomorphic language. Chapter 1 asserts that God called, saw, blessed, deliberated (vs. 26, 'Let us make'). God distributed His work over a period of six days. He rested." (38/56)

The third general difference from the critical viewpoint concerns style, vocabulary, and grammar. Upon close scrutiny, however, these "differences" leave a lot to be desired. Kitchen dismisses this difference summarily when he writes: "The stylistic differences are meaningless, and reflect the differences in detailed subject matter." (20/118)

And as Young states, "The distinctive vocabulary indicates not a particular author, but is chosen because of the peculiar contents of the chapter. It would be difficult to write in Hebrew upon these subjects without employing this particular vocabulary." (38/53–54)

Wiener points out that the critics do have some excuse for this assumption of theirs that diversity of style proves different authorship:

"The Hebrew text or the traditional explanation of the law did in fact appear to present some real difficulty or at least some justification for the contention of critics who had no special training and no qualifications for literary criticism." (36/92)

Simple logic brings Wiener to the lucid conclusion:

"Would it not be easier to suppose that 'P' could vary his language when occasion demanded than to postulate this extraordinary machinery of lists and compilers?" (36/89)

The stylistic differences are more apparent than real, and the logic employed above demonstrates effectively that style, which includes vocabulary and grammar, does not convincingly establish contradiction. C. S. Lewis, a valid critic in his own right, speaks from the "receiving end" of critical analysis and writes:

"The idea that any man or writer should be opaque to those who live in the same culture, spoke the same language, shared the same habitual imagery and unconscious assumptions, and yet be transparent to those who have none of these advantages is, in my opinion, preposterous. There is an *a priori* improbability in it which almost no argument and no evidence could counterbalance." (39/158)

Specific Differences

One objection with regard to sequence is that the initial account has creation beginning with the waters while the second account deals with creation from dry land. Cassuto cogently remarks with regard to this allegation:

"This objection, however, is valid only if we disturb the unity of the text and regard the two narratives as independent accounts; in other words, if we consider as already proven what still remains to be proven.

"If in truth, the combined sections form a continuous whole, it is clear that from the standpoint of the second section, too, creation commenced with the waters of the deep, which are mentioned at the beginning." (6/73–74)

The sequential differences with regard to the creation of man and woman are also a major point of contention, but if properly understood the problem vanishes.

In the first creation narrative, man is referred to as one creature among many and he is mentioned only as a link in the great chain of creative events. The manner of his creation is described only in general terms.

By the simple phrase "male and female created He them," we are not told how they were made or if they were created at the same time. There is only the indefinite statement that they were created.

In the second account, when the writer elaborates the story of mankind's origin, it is explained in detail how man and woman were formed respectively. This is not a matter of inconsistency, but of a general statement followed by a detailed account, which is a common literary device in ancient Semitic writing. (6/74)

The critical contention that vegetation did not appear until after the creation of man in the second account, in contradistinction to the first account when it precedes man, is another alleged problem that has a ready solution.

Pieters points out: "The writer cannot have supposed that the absence of a farmer would prevent the growth of wild grass and plants; for everyone knows the contrary. The lack of a farmer accounts for the lack of farm plants only." (26/78)

Cassuto looks at the problem from a more general standpoint and offers a very plausible explanation of why vegetation would seem to follow man in the second account:

"Here it is explained how they were planted—a general statement followed by a detailed description. What does the gardener do when he plants a new garden? Although he produces new trees from the soil, he does not create new species. Even so the Lord God did: in order to make the garden He caused good trees to grow out of its soil, of the species that He had already created on the third day." (6/76–77)

It also should be noted that, although the growth of the shrubs and sprouting of the herbs are represented here as being dependent upon the rain and the cultivation of the earth by man, it must not be understood that the words mean there was neither shrub nor herb before the creation of man. The shrub and the herb of the field do not embrace the whole of the vegetable productions of the earth. (18/77)

An interesting botanical fact is that the plants which were created on the third day are those that are capable of reproducing themselves afterwards by means of seed. This would, therefore, exclude those for which seed alone is insufficient, since they need something else in addition, something that had not yet come into the world.

There were not any thorns or thistles of the field, because Yahweh-Elohim had not caused it to rain upon the earth. The fields of grain had not yet sprung up, because there was not anyone to till the ground. Every summer, it is observed that, while the seeds of the thorns and thistles lie scattered on the ground in large numbers, not one of them springs up.

However, as soon as the rain falls, the earth is covered with thorns and thistles. As for the fields of grain, even though isolated specimens of barley and wheat do exist in a natural state, they are not found in great quantities in any one place. Fields of grain are produced only by man. (6/76)

Again, the alleged discrepancy fades under the application of logic and fact. The creation of animals after man in the second account proves a somewhat more difficult problem to resolve. However, this problem is not insurmountable, despite the critics' allegations to the contrary.

Much of the problem results over the assumption by the critics that the sequence of chapter 2 is chronological, when it never was meant to be understood in that manner, or as Young puts it, "To insist upon a chronological order in chapter 2 is to place a construction upon the writer's words that was never intended." (38/56)

Taylor Lewis notes the same thing when he states, "The trouble springs from the assuming of a chronology, and endeavoring to find it, when the chief feature of this second narrative . . . is its wholly unchronological character." (22/20)

Thus, the sequential difficulty with regard to the creation of man and animals, understood from this viewpoint, disappears. However, the problem of tense in 2:19 still gives some trouble.

Kitchen, in answer to Driver's assertion that to render the first verb in 2:19, "had formed" would be "contrary to idiom," writes:

"In Genesis 2:19, there is not explicit warrant in the text for assuming that the creation of animals here happened immediately before their naming (i.e., after man's creation); this is eisegesis, not exegesis. The proper equivalent in English for the first verb in Genesis 2:19 is the pluperfect ('had formed'). Thus, the artificial difficulty over the order of events disappears." (20/118)

The second account does not teach the creation of man before the animals. The chronological order is not what is being stressed. Chapter 2 has described the formation of Eden and the placement of Adam in the garden. It now speaks of man's condition, demonstrating his need of a helpmate for himself, and that such a helpmate was not found among the animals.

The sequence is not chronological, since there is not any justification to import the idea of time into the second chapter. The initial account of creation had already informed us of the chronological sequence; therefore, verse 19 may correctly be paraphrased, "and the Lord God having formed out of the ground every beast of the field, and every fowl of heaven, brought them unto the man." (38/56)

Kitchen develops this argument further and justifies the rendering "had formed":

"As pluperfect meaning is included in the Perfective, we cannot *a priori* deny it to contextual equivalents of the Perfective. Hebraists and others should also remember that no special pluperfect tenses exist in the Ancient Semitic Languages (or in Egyptian), this nuance being covered by prefective forms and equivalents interpreted on context as here in Hebrew." (20/119)

He further adds examples from Scripture to support this argument:

"The meaning of any Waw-Consecutive-Imperfective must be settled on context, not by appeal to abstract principles ... For Hebrew Waw-Consecutive-Imperfectives that require a pluperfect standpoint in English, cf: Exodus 4:19 (picking up 4:12, not 18); Exodus 19:2 ('having departed ... and come ... they pitched ...' picks up 17:1, not 19:1; these examples, courtesy Dr. W.J. Martin.)

"Perhaps more striking, Joshua 2:22 ('now the pursuers had sought them ...') does not continue immediately preceding verbs. I Kings 13:12 ('Now his sons had seen' does not continue or follow from 'their father said') Driver, Treatise ... p. 87, can only dispose of I Kings 13:12 by appealing to the versions." (20/118–119 N. 19)

But even if Driver's assertion that the pluperfect rendering is contrary to idiom is absolutely correct (which the above examples from Scripture tend to negate), there is still the explanation set forth by Cassuto and Archer, which gives a plausible reason for the apparent contradiction in the order of creation with regard to man and animals.

Archer concludes that the critics' reasoning is faulty in regarding the account as chronological and point out the purpose for the order:

"It is a mistake to suppose that Genesis 2 indicates the creation of the animal order as taking place after the origin of man. It only states that the particular individuals brought before Adam for naming had been especially fashioned by God for this purpose. (It does not imply that there were no animals anywhere else in the world prior to this time.)" (4/118)

Elaborating on this line of thought, and carrying his explanation of the placement of vegetation in the creative order over to the placement of animals in the order of creation, Cassuto remarks:

"We find in the second section that the Lord God formed out of the ground the beasts and the flying creatures (v. 19); whereas the first section informs us that the beasts and the flying creatures were created before man. But in this case, too, we have to be careful not to regard the words of the Bible as though they were isolated and unrelated to their context.

"According to the continuation of the passage, the Lord God's intention was to pass in review before the man all the species of animals in order that he should give them names, and endeavor to find among them a helper corresponding to him.

"The cattle, which should have been the first to be considered in this connection, are not mentioned at all among the kinds of animals that the Lord God then made. Yet we are explicitly told afterwards that Adam gave names to the cattle, the beasts and the flying creatures (v. 20).

"This implies that the cattle, owing to their nature, were already to be found in the garden with man, in agreement with the first section. But in order that all the various kinds of beasts and flying creatures that were scattered through the length and breadth of the world should also be represented in Adam's abode, the Lord God formed, from the soil of the garden, beasts and flying creatures of every type previously created, and He brought them to the man." (6/77)

Again, better solutions are found to the apparent problems between the two chapters than those posed by the critics.

Unity of Plan

The unity of plan of Genesis is not at issue, but when and how the plan came is. As was noted earlier in chapter 2 of this discussion, the critics recognize this unity but attribute it to "P," and then postulate that the unifying phrase originally stood before chapter 1 of Genesis and was transposed by a redactor.

However, the formula, "These are the generations," occurs ten times in the Book of Genesis, and in every instance but in 2:4 it is indisputable the title of the section to which it is prefixed. (14/9)

The critics realize that 2:4 in its present position refutes their theory, hence the parcelling of the verse. They realize the way it stands, it rivets the second chapter to the first in more ways than one. Unfortunately, it could never have been the title of chapter 1, since the heavens and earth must first be created before its generations can be spoken of.

The phrase in Genesis 2:4 does not introduce the account of creation of heaven and earth. Therefore we learn from this key phrase that 2:4ff does not profess to present an account of creation. Rather than being a duplicate account of the creation, verses 4–26 present the grand theme of the formation of man and the first stage of human history. (38/54–55)

If the critics are correct in their analysis that the phrase in chapter 2 belongs in front of chapter 1, the title there would stand in no relation to the subsequent titles of the book. Grass and trees and animals supply no stepping-stone to the next title, "The Generations of Adam."

Adam is not introduced until 1:26, and he is merely mentioned in the general scheme of things. There is no record of what befell him or his family, as would be expected; therefore, 2:5–4:26 is necessary. The clause joins the first two chapters and cannot be removed by any critical device.

It is, therefore, quite clear in this case that the clause, "These are the generations," does not refer to the preceding section, but to what follows, and that it introduces a new subject. Since every other place this heading is used it precedes a section, the same should be the case with 2:4.

Toledoth nowhere else expresses the idea of creation; rather, it always introduces an ensuing account of the offspring of an ancestor through the generations which descended from him. It, therefore, becomes obvious that in Genesis 2 we are dealing with an account of the offspring of heaven and earth, namely, Adam and Eve.

This occurred after the initial creation had already taken place. (28/24) Thus, the internal evidence of the unity of plan in itself declares the critics' analysis to be false in this regard, as well as the others. There was an evident intention to harmony which precludes the critics' assumption of contrariety.

There is a minority view regarding the clause, "These are the generations," to the effect that the formula is a concluding sentence "to point back to the origins of the family history." (37/50)

Wiseman, after his examination of the new archaeological data, concluded:

"The Book of Genesis was originally written on tablets in the ancient script of the time, by the Patriarchs who were intimately concerned with the events related, and whose names are clearly stated. Moreover, Moses, the compiler and editor of the Book, as we now have it, plainly directs attention to the source of his information." (37/8)

Henry Morris (*The Book of Beginnings*, p. 27) concurs with Wiseman's analysis and points out that the events recorded prior to the clause "all took place *before*, not after, the death of the individuals so named, and so could in each case have been accessible to them." This view of compiled documents is a plausible alternative explanation of the composition of Genesis.

As Pieters noted, "The writer of Genesis may have used earlier documents which all historians do, or . . . he may have found the entire first chapter already in existence, written by some other hand, and incorporated it into his book. This would not be at all inconsistent with the divine inspiration of his work . . ." (26/73–74)

If true that Genesis is made up, in good part, of documents compiled into a single book, whose concluding sentence, "These are the generations of," means origins and therefore refers back to what was just written, instead of a unifying formula which introduces what follows and means "offspring," this would eliminate the problems of the first chapter not having a formula title and the inconsistency of having the clause conclude the first chapter and begin all the other sections. Either explanation, however, is more reasonable and natural than the critic's assertions of contrariety.

Mythological Derivation

To the final major contention of the critical school that the creation accounts were derived from mythological sources, the harmonists point to both logical criteria and new discoveries to refute the contention. Harrison notes the uniqueness of the account and writes, "The first of these accounts is unique for its dignified monotheism and non-mythological nature." (33/1022)

Kitchen points to the methodological weakness in this contention:

"The common assumption that the Hebrew account is simply a purged and simplified version of the Babylonian legend . . . is fallacious on methodological grounds. In Ancient Near East, the rule is that simple accounts or traditions may give rise (by accretion and embellishment) to elaborate legends, but not vice versa.

"In the Ancient Orient, legends were not simplified or turned into pseudo-history (historicized) as has been assumed for early Genesis." (20/89)

The sequential similarities between the Enuma Elish and chapter 1 of Genesis give rise to the contention that they were derived from the same mythological source. In the two stories, the following events take place in the same order: the creation of the firmament, the creation of dry land, the creation of the luminaries, and the creation of man. Both the Genesis account and the Enuma Elish begin with the watery chaos and end with the Lord or the gods at rest. (9/53)

However, Jack Finegan notes, "It must be recognized that the differences between Enuma Elish and the Old Testament are far more important than the similarities." (9/53)

Harrison amplifies the situation:

"From the time when George Smith first introduced the Gilgamesh Epic to English readers, it was commonly assumed that the original material underlying Genesis 1 as a whole was the Babylonian Creation Epic known as Enuma Elish, even though Wellhausen himself could discover no mythological ingredients in Genesis 1 save for chaos, a view that his followers either repudiated or ignored.

"A more careful study of similarities and differences, however, has made it evident that resemblances between the Babylonian and Israelite cosmogonies are not as close as had been imagined previously." (15/555)

Kitchen carries this line of thinking much farther and points out the vast disparity in the underlying aims of the two accounts:

"The aims of Genesis 1 and 2 and of the so-called 'Babylonian Creation' (Enuma Elish) are quite distinct. Genesis aims to portray the sole God as sovereign creator, whereas the primary purpose of Enuma Elish is to exalt the chief god of the Babylonian pantheon.

"The contrast between the monotheism and simplicity of the Hebrew account and the polytheism and elaboration of the Mesopotamian epic is obvious to any reader." (20/88–89)

The mythological source derivation was a hasty contention born out of inadequate evidence and lack of logical attention to the text. More careful study shows it to be without basis in fact; logic shows it to be more likely that myth was born or developed from Genesis than the other way around. This contention of the critical school also carries no significant weight to proving contradiction.

Analysis and Conclusions

Having dealt with the specific discrepancies, and being able to conclude that for the most part the discrepancies are illusory, and where they are more real, as with Genesis 2:19, they can be better explained without recourse to alleging contradiction, it is necessary now to examine the presuppositional basis of the critics' case, and their methodology.

There are certain features of historical inquiry that the critical school would have done well to keep in mind. The first is that "in translating any ancient text, the first assumption is that the writer intended it to make sense; a rendering or exegesis that imports a contradiction is unsatisfactory." (20/118 N.19)

Coleridge provides an excellent criterion for approaching a document. "When we meet an apparent error in a good author, we are to presume ourselves ignorant of his understanding, until we are certain that we understand his ignorance." (1/125)

Long ago, Aristotle set forth a basis for evaluating documents which must be taken into account. He said that the "benefit of the doubt is to be given to the document itself, not arrogated by the critic to himself." (25/47)

These basic criteria, as set forth by Aristotle, Coleridge, and Kitchen, underlie all sound historical inquiry into ancient documents. However, further examination will show the failure of the critics' case in their approach and basic presuppositions.

It must be kept in mind that the radical view of the critic is based upon the subjective whim of the interpreters, not upon any objective external evidence. This is evident as Pieters explains the methodological assumptions of the critical school:

"This hypothesis . . . is to the effect that there were . . . two distinct books, now lost, setting forth the ancient history of that people. The theory is that someone took these two histories, and without concerning himself much about their differences, or even contradictions, made one new book of them by weaving them together, taking sometimes a passage from the one and sometimes from the other.

"To be sure, no one has ever seen any copy of either of the two works alleged to have existed, nor is there any reference to them in any ancient literature, nor was it so much as suspected by the learned Jewish scholars that they had ever existed; but modern Jewish scholars claim to have discovered them by analysis of the text now in our possession.

"They believe that they can tell even in minute detail which separate verses in any chapter were written by the 'Elohist' and which by the 'Jehovist.' (He refers to the result as the 'literary crazy-quilt.')." (26/72–73)

The critical school, instead of saying, "Here is a natural and sensible account which is obviously a unity," often divide it between sources, alleging that the parts missing in one contained exactly the same information in the exact parts of the other. No matter how improbable this may appear, it is hardly possible to produce any reason that will convince the critics. Yet an unbiased person will have no doubts when he examines the facts. (36/114)

The critics force the text to conform to their subjective view. Instead of adapting their theories to the evidence presented by the text, they insist upon reconstructing the text in accordance with their own theory. The advantage of a method such as this is that anyone can triumphantly establish whatever he desires to set out to prove. (14/36)

It is a very simple thing to take two narratives or two parts of the same narrative, which have various points in common but describe different transactions, and lay them alongside of each other and point out their lack of correspondence. The work of the critics consists in identifying distinct things in the accounts from which different traditions, they claim, can be seen.

These discrepant accounts, they contend, cannot be by the same author, but are from different documents. However, the simple fact is that there is not reason or occasion to come to such an extraordinary conclusion.

It makes much more sense to contend that the writer has finished one part of his story, has proceeded to another and, as might well be expected, does not put in detail again that which he had immediately detailed before. (14/7–8)

Kitchen concurs with this analysis of the methodology:

"Internal agreement of rearranged literary material is readily achieved if contrary data are emended away, and agreement with the 'history' is equally easily attained if data in the historical books have also been duly 'adjusted' to fit in with views of what Israel's history ought to have been. Hence, this kind of general approach has no scientific basis and is for that reason unacceptable." (20/116)

The "two creation accounts," which brought about this whole scholarly journey, now are used as proof texts of the theory that was born out of the theory to explain the differences between the "two accounts."

Simply stated, the critics are saying that (1) the first two chapters of Genesis are contradictory because they came from two different documents, and (2) the documentary hypothesis is proved by the existence of double narratives and contradictions; for example, the first two chapters of Genesis.

However, despite the related elements, the two sections in question cannot be held to be either duplicate accounts or even genuine parallels in the commonly accepted sense, for the initial account speaks in completely general terms, while the second narrative deals from a different standpoint with a specific pair of individuals dwelling in a single locality. (15/555)

The work of the critics has had a destructive influence over the years. Many of their theories consist of building veritable castles in the air which are totally devoid of any solid foundation.

Every support of the critics' case can be shown to be no support at all and, to use Kravitz' words, "might rightfully be described as a would-be answer to a would-be question about an imaginary explanation of a non-existent text." (21/49–50)

(He was referring specifically to the critics' cavilling over Genesis 2:4.) Their case fails in presuppositions, in evidence and in methodology, and it is notable that when the critics get to that point, all else failing them, they postulate the redactor.

Sometimes the critics sweep aside difficulties by asserting that the redactor altered the name of God. Other times they insist that the text is evidently corrupt. However, neither of these suppositions has any basis outside of the mind of the theorists.

Their hypothesis supposedly is derived from the phenomena in the text as it stands; but if those phenomena do not suit their hypothesis, they are cast off as worthless. If the text is corrupt how can anyone trust the hypothesis that is derived from it? (30/120)

Allis makes a brilliant observation in this same vein that the critical school conveniently overlooks: "It is to be noted, therefore, that every appeal to the redactor is a tacit admission on the part of the critics that their theory breaks down at that point." (2/39)

The admission of a final redactor is, therefore, fatal to the critical assertion of contradictions that are totally irreconcilable. A man of such tremendous ability as the redactor must have possessed would certainly have seen the contradictions if they were as blatant as the critics contend, and he would have removed them. (30/127)

The critics' case has been difficult to organize and answer along logical, consistent lines, which in itself is evidence that their arguments are illogical and inconsistent. As has been shown, the critics' case has no external evidence to support it from archaeological discoveries, or form the resulting increase in knowledge of ancient Near Eastern literary styles.

Wiseman aptly noted this when he stated, "These conjectures would never have seen the light of day had scholars of that time been in possession of modern archaeological knowledge." (37/10)

BIBLIOGRAPHY

1. Allis, Oswald T., *The Five Books of Moses*, Philadelphia, The Presbyterian and Reformed Publishing Company, 1969, 355 pp.
2. _____, *The Old Testament, Its Claims and Its Critics*, New Jersey, The Presbyterian and Reformed Publishing Company, 1972, 509 pp.
3. Anderson, George W., *A Critical Introduction to the Old Testament*, London, Gerald Duckworth & Co. Ltd., 1959, 260 pp.
4. Archer, Gleason Jr., *A Survey of Old Testament Introduction*, Chicago, Moody Press, 1964, 1974, 528 pp.
5. Carroll, B. H., *The Book of Genesis*, ed. J. B. Cranfill, New York, Fleming H. Revell Company, 1913, 451 pp.
6. Cassuto, Umberto, *The Documentary Hypothesis*, 1st Eng. ed., Jerusalem Magnes Press, 1961, 117 pp.
7. Driver, S. R., *The Book of Genesis*, 8th ed., London, Methuen & Co., 1911, 420 pp.
8. _____, *Introduction to the Literature of the Old Testament*, New York, Charles Scribner's Sons, 1913, 577 pp. Ninth Edition Revised
9. Finegan, Jack, *Light from the Ancient Past*, Princeton University Press, 1946, 500 pp.
10. Frazer, James George, *Folklore in the Old Testament*, New York, MacMillain Company, 1923, 476 pp.
11. Fretheim, Terence E., *Creation, Fall and Flood*, Minneapolis, Augsburg Publishing House, 1969, 127 pp.
12. Gaster, Theodor H., *Myth, Legend and Custom in the Old Testament*, 2 vols., New York, Harper and Row, 1975.
13. Green, William H., *The Higher Criticism of the Pentateuch*, New York, Chas. Scribner's Sons, 1895, 184 pp.
14. _____, *The Unity of the Book of Genesis*, New York, Scribner, 1895, 581 pp.
15. Harrison, R. K., *Introduction to the Old Testament*, Grand Rapids, Wm. B. Eerdmans Publishing Company, 1969.
16. James, A. Gordon, *Creation Stories of Genesis*, London, Student Christian Movement, 1927, 182 pp.
17. Kalisch, M. M., *Genesis*, London, Longman, Brown, Green, Longman and Roberts, 1858, 531 pp.
18. Keil, C. F., and Delitzsch, F., *Biblical Commentary on the Old Testament*, William B. Eerdmans Publishing Company, 1949.
19. Kidner, Derek, *Genesis: An Introduction and Commentary*, Chicago, Inter-Varsity Press, 1966, 191 pp.
20. Kitchen, K. A., *Ancient Orient and the Old Testament*, Chicago, Inter-Varsity Press, 1966, 191 pp.
21. Kravitz, Nathan, *Genesis: A New Interpretation of the First Three Chapters*, New York, Philosophical Library, 1967, 83 pp.
22. Lange, John Peter, *Commentary on the Holy Scriptures*, 25 vols., trans. and ed. Philip Schaff, Grand Rapids, Zondervan Publishing House, (no date).
23. Leupold, Herbert Carl, *Exposition of Genesis*, Grand Rapids, Baker Book House, 1958.
24. Martin, W. J., *Stylistic Criteria and the Analysis of the Pentateuch*, London, Tyndale Press, 1955, 23 pp.

25. McDowell, Josh, *More Evidence That Demands a Verdict*, Arrowhead Springs Campus Crusade for Christ, 1975, 365 pp.
26. Pieters, Albertus, *Notes on Genesis*, Grand Rapids, William B. Eerdmans Publishing Company, 11943, 179 pp.
27. Plummer, A., Driver, S. R., Briggs, G. A., ed., *The International Critical Commentary*, Edinburgh, T & T Clark, 1912, 552 pp.
28. Pratt, H. B., *Studies in the Book of Genesis*, New York, American Tract Society, 1904, 530 pp.
29. Rad, Gerhard von, *Genesis*, Philadelphia, Westminster Press, 1972, 434 pp.
30. Raven, John Howard, *Old Testament Introduction*, rev., New York, Fleming H. Revell Company, 1910, 363 pp.
31. Rowley, H. H., *The Growth of the Old Testament*, London, Hutchinson & Co., 1950, 192 pp.
32. Schedl, Claus, *History of the Old Testament*, 5 vols., New York, Alba House, 1973.
33. Tenney, Merrill C., ed., *Zondervan Pictorial Encyclopedia of Bible*, vol. I, Zondervan, 1975, Article "Creation" by R. K. Harrison.
34. Weill, Alexandre, *Le Pentateuque Selon Moise*, Paris, Felix Alcan, 186, 214 pp.
35. West, James King, *Introduction to the Old Testament*, New York, The Macmillan Company, 1971, 546 pp.
36. Wiener, Harold M., *The Origin of the Pentateuch*, Oberlin Bibliotheca Sacra Company, 1910, 152 pp.
37. Wiseman, P. J., *New Discoveries in Babylonia about Genesis*, 3rd ed., London, Marshall, Morgan & Scott, (no date) 150 pp.
38. Young, E. J., *An Introduction to the Old Testament*, Grand Rapids, Eerdmans Publishing Company, 1949, 434 pp.
39. Lewis, C. S. "Modern Theology and Biblical Criticism," *Christian Reflections*, Wlater Hooper, ed., Grand Rapids, William B. Eerdmans, 1967, 152–166 pp.
40. Stewart, Donald, Adapted from Masters Dissertation, *The Unified Account of Creation*, Presented to the Department of Old Testament and Semetics, Talbot Theological Seminary, La Mirada, California, 1979.

Have You Heard of the Four Spiritual Laws?

Just as there are physical laws that govern the physical universe, so are there spiritual laws which govern your relationship with God.

LAW ONE

GOD *LOVES* YOU, AND OFFERS A WONDERFUL *PLAN* FOR YOUR LIFE.

God's Love

"For God so loved the world, that He gave His only begotten Son, that whoever believes in Him should not perish, but have eternal life" (John 3:16).

God's Plan

(Christ speaking) "I came that they might have life, and might have it abundantly" (that it might be full and meaningful) (John 10:10).

Why is it that most people are not experiencing the abundant life? Because . . .

LAW TWO

MAN IS *SINFUL* AND *SEPARATED* FROM GOD. THEREFORE, HE CANNOT KNOW AND EXPERIENCE GOD'S LOVE AND PLAN FOR HIS LIFE.

Man Is Sinful

"For all have sinned and fall short of the glory of God" (Romans 3:23).

Man was created to have fellowship with God; but, because of his stubborn self-will, he chose to go his own independent way and fellowship with God was broken. This self-will, characterized by an attitude of active rebellion or passive indifference, is evidence of what the Bible calls sin.

Man Is Separated

"For the wages of sin is death" (spiritual separation from God) (Romans 6:23).

God is holy and man is sinful. A great gulf separates the two . . . man is continually trying to reach God and the abundant life through his own efforts, such as a good life, philosophy, or religion.

The third law explains the only way to bridge this gulf.

LAW THREE

JESUS CHRIST IS GOD'S *ONLY* PROVISION FOR MAN'S SIN. THROUGH HIM YOU CAN KNOW AND EXPERIENCE GOD'S LOVE AND PLAN FOR YOUR LIFE.

He Died in Our Place
"But God demonstrates His own love toward us, in that while we were yet sinners, Christ died for us" (Romans 5:8).

He Rose from the Dead
"Christ died for our sins . . . He was buried . . . He was raised on the third day, according to the Scriptures . . . He appeared to Peter, then to the twelve. After that He appeared to more than five hundred . . ." (I Corinthians 15:3–6).

He Is the Only Way to God
"Jesus said to him, I am the way, and the truth, and the life; no one comes to the Father, but through Me'" (John 14:6).

God has bridged the gulf which separates us from God by sending His Son, Jesus Christ, to die on the cross in our place to pay the penalty for our sins.

It is not enough just to know these three laws . . .

LAW FOUR

WE MUST INDIVIDUALLY *RECEIVE* JESUS CHRIST AS SAVIOR AND LORD; THEN WE CAN KNOW AND EXPERIENCE GOD'S LOVE AND PLAN FOR OUR LIVES.

We Must Receive Christ
"But as many as received Him, to them He gave the right to become children of God, even to those who believe in His name" (John 1:12).

We Receive Christ through Faith
"For by grace you have been saved through faith; and that no of yourselves, it is the gift of God; not as a result of works, that no one should boast" (Ephesians 2:8, 9).

When We Receive Christ, We Experience a New Birth
(Read John 3:1–8).

We Receive Christ by Personal Invitation
(Christ is speaking) "Behold, I stand at the door and knock; if any one hears My voice and opens the door, I will come in to him" (Revelation 3:20).

Receiving Christ involves turning from self to God (repentance) and trusting Christ to come into our lives to forgive our sins and to make us the kind of person He wants us to be. Just to agree intellectually that Jesus Christ is the Son of God and that He died on the cross for our sins is not enough. Nor is it enough to have an emotional experience. We receive Jesus Christ by faith, as an act of the will.

These two circles represent two kinds of lives:

SELF-DIRECTED LIFE
S - Self on the throne
✝ - Christ is outside the life
• - Interests are directed by self, often resulting in discord and frustration

CHRIST- DIRECTED LIFE
✝ - Christ is in the life
S - Self is yielding to Christ
• - Interests are directed by Christ, resulting in harmony with God's plan

Which circle best represents your life?
Which circle would you like to have represent your life?
The following explains how you can receive Christ:

YOU CAN RECEIVE CHRIST RIGHT NOW BY FAITH THROUGH PRAYER

(Prayer is talking with God)

God knows your heart and is not so concerned with your words as He is with the attitude of your heart. The following is a suggested prayer:

"Lord Jesus, I need You. Thank You for dying on the cross for my sins. I open the door of my life and receive You as my Savior and Lord. Thank You for forgiving my sins and giving me eternal life. Make me the kind of person you want me to be."

Does this prayer express the desire of your heart?
If it does, pray this prayer right now, and Christ will come into your life, as He promised.

About the Authors

Josh McDowell is considered one of America's foremost defenders of the Christian faith. He is a graduate of Wheaton College and Talbot Theological Seminary and author of over twenty-six books, including *Evidence That Demands a Verdict, Handbook of Today's Religions, His Image . . . My Image, The Secret of Loving, and Why Wait?*

Don Stewart is a graduate of Talbot Theological Seminary and has co-authored several books with Josh McDowell.

Let's Stay In Touch!

If you have grown personally as a result of this material, we should stay in touch. You will want to continue in your Christian growth, and to help your faith become even stronger, our team is constantly developing new materials.

We publish a monthly newsletter called **5 Minutes with Josh** which will:

1) tell you about those new materials as they become available,
2) answer your tough questions,
3) give creative tips on being an effective parent,
4) let you know our ministry needs, and
5) keep you up-to-date on my speaking schedule (so you can pray).

If you would like to receive this publication, simply fill out the coupon below and send it in. By special arrangement **5 Minutes with Josh** will come to you regularly — <u>no charge</u>.

Let's keep in touch!

Josh

Yes! I want to receive the free subscription to **5 Minutes with JOSH**

Name_____

Address_____

City_____State_____Zip _____

Mail to: Josh McDowell Ministry, **5 Minutes with Josh**, Box 1000, Dallas, TX 75221